FUTURE KIND

FUTURE KIND

Essays on raising the generation
our world needs

Edited by
Elisabeth Johnson

radiate

radiate

Radiate Publishing
PO Box 3517, Mornington,
Victoria 3931, Australia.

www.radiatepublishing.com.au
enquiries@radiatepublishing.com.au

First published 2019
Text © individual contributors 2019
Design and typography © Radiate Publishing 2019
Cover illustration © Radiate Publishing 2019

Printed in Australia

ISBN 978 0 6487055 0 5 (print)
ISBN 978 0 6487055 1 2 (ebook)

All rights reserved. This book is copyright. Apart from any use permitted under the Copyright Act 1968 and subsequent amendments, and any exceptions permitted under the current statutory licence scheme administered by Copyright Agency Limited (www.copyright.com.au), no part may be reproduced, stored in a retrieval system or transmitted by any means or process by any means whatsoever without the prior written permission of the publisher.

Websites and printed material referred to in this book are not under the control of the publisher or any individual contributor unless specified and they are not responsible for the accuracy of the contents therein. None of the information or advice in this book should be regarded as legal advice in any way and is provided for general guidance only. Formal advice should always be sought from a qualified practitioner in regard to legal or medical matters.

A catologuing-in-data entry for this book is available from the National Library of Australia: https://catalogue.nla.gov.au/

Contents

Preface *Elisabeth Johnson* vi

Contributors ix

1. How to parent while saving the world *Heidi Edmonds* 1
2. Facing the realities of climate change *Susie Burke & Anne Sanson* 13
3. Developing climate consciousness *Rachel Forgasz* 27
4. Connecting with nature *Melinda Bito* 43
5. Connection — the power of 'us' *Robin Grille* 49
6. Trust: the currency of childhood *Brigitte Kupfer* 68
7. The future of intelligence *Ricci-Jane Adams* 76
8. Sacred activism and being an ally *Phoebe Mwanza* 88
9. A colourful upbringing *Naomi Kissiedu* 103
10. Indigenous perspectives *Larissa Behrendt* 113
11. Feelings can be wrong *Nelly Thomas* 117
12. Safe enough to innovate *Anna Lidstone* 132
13. Leadership in children *Marilou Coombe* 149
14. Responsibility parenting *Andrew Lines* 158

Index 176

Preface

Elisabeth Johnson

NOT LONG after becoming a parent five years ago I found myself asking how I could ensure my daughter grew to be a confident and compassionate adult. A focus on concepts such as mindfulness, and emotional intelligence-based so-called 'soft skills' for children were becoming increasingly mainstream, but in subsequent years, as the global political, economic and environmental situations began to feel increasingly dire, a deeper exploration was needed.

Profound cultural change is needed, yet how do we raise a generation who will effect this significant positive change in our world? And how do we effectively equip them to handle these changes, including the potential chaos they may encounter during this period of global transition?

With these questions in mind, I set out to compile a collection of ideas and advice from an interesting variety of academics, social commentators, parenting mentors, and of course, established authors, offering their own area of expertise and insight.

My aim has been to provide a holistic collection aligned with the three dimensions of engagement in the process of cultural transformation described by eco-philosopher and scholar Joanne Macy: "1) actions to slow the damage to Earth and its beings; 2) analysis of structural causes and creation of structural alternatives; and 3) a fundamental shift in worldview and values." (Macy and Young Brown, 1998)

There are so many aspects to these emerging cultural shifts. The list of topics relating them to raising children seems endless and I could easily have continued to pursue contributors ad infinitum. Gender and sexuality, refugee-ism, Indigenous reconciliation, effects of late stage capitalism; these are also important topics. My hope is that this anthology nevertheless covers the crux of many underlying (and more explicit) issues plaguing our society, and themes found within the chapters can apply to a range of circumstances.

In order to achieve better ways of living as a society, our children need to be well equipped with the mental, social, and emotional skills to navigate the breakdown of the current systems, and the fall out effects for themselves and fellow individuals and communities. As we hint in the anthology title 'Future Kind,' empathy, loving kindness, and respect (along with an understanding of intersectionality and egalitarianism) will be key to successfully improving our existence on this planet, for all living things. Kindness is an antidote to fear, it underpins the building of community, and it promotes a deeper understanding of our interconnectedness.

Finding the balance between raising kind humans and steeling them against the harshness of our world is an unending challenge. And the current (or perhaps, continuing) state of play leaves many of us experiencing anger, grief, and anxiety. Indeed, one author pulled out of the anthology when she found herself too overwhelmed by the topic; and there were times when, after reading many climate science reports and articles, I myself wondered if the book ought to be called "*Future, What Future?*"

So, what I also want to impart through this collection is **hope**, for what Charles Eisenstein calls "the more beautiful world our hearts know is possible" (2013). We need to ground ourselves in an acknowledgement and understanding that our separation is an illusion — whether accepting it for ourselves as inter-beings connected to all other living things (in other words, we **are** nature), or the ways in which all these topics are deeply interrelated and intractable;

no one issue sits in isolation from the other. Embracing this allows us to accept that "every act counts, [and] every thought and emotion counts too" (Chödrön, 2005). As parents this means that even the small everyday moments with our children offer huge potential to effect positive change, not just in how we guide our children, but through our own self awareness, growth, and healing.

Although you will find much overlap and intertwinement amongst the chapters, I'm sure it goes without saying that each of the author's views are their own, and not reflective of the other contributing authors (or me) by default. However, I would like to acknowledge the work of the following writers and activists (in addition to all the *Future Kind* contributing authors of course) for expanding my understanding and views in the areas of anti-racism, subconscious bias, alternative economics, new paradigm thinking, and sacred activism, and who subsequently shaped the direction of this book: Sharyn Holmes, Layla F Saad, Polly Higgins, Charles Eisenstein, and George Monbiot.

On that note, I also wish to thank my father (and Radiate Publishing co-founder) for his extraordinary mentorship, my husband for his continued support, and my two amazing daughters — ultimately all that I do is for you two, and your future.

References

Macy, J & Young Brown, M 1998, *Coming Back to Life: Practices to Reconnect Our Lives, Our World,* New Society Publishers, Gabriola Island, British Columbia, Canada.

Chödrön, P 2005, *When Things Fall Apart: Heart Advice for Difficult Times,* Shambhala Publications, Boston.

Eisenstein, C 2013, *The More Beautiful World Our Hearts Know Is Possible,* North Atlantic Books, Berkeley, California.

Contributors

Ricci-Jane Adams is the principal of the Institute for Intuitive Intelligence and the author of bestselling *Spiritually Fierce*, the formula for an activated intuition. She has a PhD from the University of Melbourne, and has spent more than 25 years devoted to her spiritual awakening. She is also a qualified Transpersonal Counsellor.

Larissa Behrendt is a Eualeyai/Kamillaroi woman. She is the Professor of Law and Director of Research at the Jumbunna Indigenous House of Learning at the University of Technology, Sydney. Prof. Behrendt is admitted to the Supreme Court of the ACT and NSW as a barrister and is a member of a number of boards. She is the author of several books on Indigenous legal issues and was named as 2009 NAIDOC Person of the Year.

Melinda Bito is the founder of Eco Explorers and Australia's first eco toy store and has been a huge advocate of sustainability, child-led play and learning for more than 12 years. Before becoming a parent she worked in Africa with orphaned chimpanzees and as an advocate for endangered wildlife.

Susie Burke is a psychologist, writer, climate change campaigner and parent, currently working in private practice in Castlemaine, Victoria, and raising bike riders, school strikers and fruit trees. She has a PhD in psychology and is a Fellow of the Australian Psychological Society. Susie is author of the *Climate Change Empowerment Handbook* and other articles and resources on the psychology of climate change.

Marilou Coombe is a coach, mentor, author, yoga teacher, and workshop and retreat facilitator. Born in Lebanon, Marilou moved to Australia aged 10-years without speaking English, which had a lasting impact on building her resilience and creating the life that she now lives. Being the mother of two 'divine' energetic young boys has been her big defining moment of change in taking action to have a more fulfilling life, and she is passionate about helping families achieve the same. Marilou has a bachelor's degree in social science, a Certificate IV in training, and coaching training including NLP, and enjoys working on mindset and gaining clarity about all aspects concerning mind, body and soul.

Heidi Edmonds is the mother of two young girls and lives in Brisbane, Queensland. She has a PhD in environmental science and is a freelance researcher and writer focused on climate resilience and solutions.. She is also co-founder of Australian Parents for Climate Action.

Rachel Forgasz is a senior lecturer in the Faculty of Education at Monash University in Melbourne where she teaches and writes about the influence of emotion, agency, and embodiment on teaching and learning. Her current research explores how to prepare teachers to work with young people in the context of global climate crisis.

Robin Grille is a psychologist, parenting educator and international speaker. He is the author of *Parenting for a Peaceful World*, *Heart to Heart Parenting*, and the forthcoming *Inner Child Journeys*. Robin's work is animated by his belief that humanity's future is dependent on how we collectively relate to our children.

Elisabeth Johnson is raising two young daughters with her husband in coastal Victoria. Her career has included trade and academic publishing, freelance design work, and e-commerce endeavours. She currently enjoys focussing her energy on a number of writing, design and community projects related to mental health, climate justice, and holistic parenting.

Naomi Kissiedu is married to an Australian, and has three beautiful multi-racial children. Naomi wrote a series of Children's books — *The Colourful Life* series — and their success led to a number of focus pieces on SBS *World News* and Al Jazerra's *The Stream* and a TEDx talk: *Are you the nanny?*

Brigitte Kupfer has been engaged in cultural and social change projects since her teenage years in Germany. She has been a psychologist and psychotherapist and now co-creates intergenerational learning and healing spaces. As an advocate for de-schooling and peer mentoring networks she supports parents in their role as evolutionary transition leaders.

Anna Lidstone is a Creativity and Innovation Consultant, working with organisations to facilitate '21st Century Thinking.' She received her PhD from the University of Toronto and is certified in a wide range of innovation methodologies. She is also a professional writer. Anna is Australian/English/Canadian, and currently lives in Brisbane.

Andrew Lines is a teacher and educational consultant whose programs and resources (*The Rite Journey*, *The Rite Journey Parenting Plan*, *Habits of Heart*, *Man Made* and *Woman Wise*) serve teachers, parents and communities by empowering them to self sufficiently and sustainably grow responsible, resilient, respectful and resourceful children and adolescents.

Phoebe Mwanza is Zambian-born and Zimbabwean-raised who is an Australian Diversity, Inclusion & Equity Consultant. She works as a lawyer, specifically in the area of human rights and anti-discrimination law. She is also the host of *The Griot Podcast* and a writer and speaker on social justice issues.

Ann Sanson's academic research has mainly focused on understanding the role of child, family and community characteristics for healthy child and adolescent development. Her current focus is on the impacts of the climate crisis on children and youth and how to best support parents and young people in dealing with it.

Nelly Thomas was a popular stand-up comedian for 16 years but has now traded the stage for the quiet life as an author and media personality. She was listed as one of Australia's "most innovative thinkers" in *The Age* newspaper and was featured on the ABC television's *Big Ideas: The Smartest Stuff*.

1

How to parent

while saving the world from climate catastrophe

Heidi Edmonds

TODAY, AS SHE has several other times, Lucinda, who is five-years-old, mentioned that she did not think Winter would ever come again. It was too hot. A pretty mid-Autumn had comfortably placed itself where Winter used to be, and I felt so deeply compelled to stop, look around, and admire the beauty of this moment. Because it was deeply, simply, complexly, and wonderfully beautiful. With a cool garden my girls can play in in the afternoon. With a sky full of patchy colours from the storm clouds that are seemingly a new, permanent fixture this Winter.

I remember when Lucinda was born, reading Steve Biddulph's *Raising Girls* (2013) in my armchair as I breastfed her late at night. I had very little time for social media or for talking with friends except when they visited. And how her May birth was amidst cold, crisp days. Just five years ago. I've managed to find more time to do things other than just parent, but this mild, barely-existent Winter has me spellbound and a little bit scared.

Last summer, when the air conditioning failed in January, we were blessed with coolish weather while the rest of Australia recovered from a

40°C+ heatwave. A week without air conditioning was frustrating, but I was so thankful that our own hot weather here in Brisbane (or Meanjin, our city's indigenous name) book-ended the cool weather when the air conditioner was on the blink. Otherwise, in our old Queenslander, with a thin and relatively un-insulated roof, it would have been baking, devastatingly hot and we would have had to stay with my mum for the week until it was fixed. Because, in the summer, air conditioning repairers are so in demand you have to book a week in advance, I plan to invest in two air conditioning units when finances allow. The portable air conditioner we bought in the interim while we waited for the new installation only shaved off a degree or two.

Love for my children was the force that called me to act on the climate crisis

I awoke to the climate emergency the year that my Stella, who is now three-years-old, was born. Up until that time, I, an environmental scientist, had a general understanding that climate change was a concern, a big concern, a very hard to solve concern, one that our governments would surely tackle; it seemed far off and unlikely to affect me. I was so busy, with starting and then finishing my environmental science PhD, with working, with coping with broken relationships, with making new friends, with making music about broken relationships, with falling in love with my husband, with learning how to raise a baby and then a child, and then a family, that when my engineering mentor David, suggested I wrap up my PhD (which seemed never-ending at the time) and focus my energies on protecting the climate I just brushed this request off until later, until I was ready, until I was finished.

The year Stella was born, David sent me an invitation to sign a petition, asking Australia to declare a climate emergency. A man I knew called Steve Posselt was riding and lugging a kayak along dried out rivers to Canberra where the petition would be delivered. It aimed for 100,000 signatures to have a good chance of being debated in federal parliament. I think it reached around 18,000 signatures. But I signed it. And I read this strange and cumbersome language that said that we needed to mobilise on climate like we were in a world war. It said that the impacts of climate change were urgent and could affect this generation of kids. I dismissed it to a point. It seemed a bit extreme.

But then as I pushed my little girls in their double-sized pram around the streets of my slice of Brisbane, the sun, renowned for its heat, beat on my back and it felt hotter than I had ever remembered. Hotter and more persistent than the heat waves of Leumeah in Sydney's south west when as a child in the 1980s, my grandma would run a cold bath to cool me down.

And so I started to read. I read a few scientific articles, but mostly I read news articles about the state of the climate, the urgency of taking action, what 1°C to 4°C warming might look like. How 4°C could mean the end of human civilisation. What this warming might mean for my little girls. I read about how the last ice age was only 4°C cooler than pre-industrial times, and 4°C warming could lead to human civilisation fraying. Even about 2°C warming is going to mess with the food my kids will be able to eat, and about how quickly we need to roll out renewables and find more sustainable ways of living. About how important it is to talk out about climate change, because not enough people are talking about it.

I shared what I learnt to *Facebook* and then later in blog articles. I discovered *Twitter* was a great platform for seeking out expert advice and discovering new perspectives. I joined Citizens Climate Lobby and met my federal member of parliament and others. I helped set up a climate advocacy group for parents called Australian Parents for Climate Action. I learned how to speak about climate with adults and children (in age appropriate ways, in line with the guidelines from the Australian Psychological Society) and I developed my own solutions-focused advocacy style. In the midst of this, first Zero Hour in the USA and then Greta Thunberg in Sweden, inspired movements led by high school students that showed the world how to talk, simply, and fearlessly, about the threat of the climate crisis.

Australian school strikers inspired by Greta Thunberg eloquently showed the world that awareness of climate change as a threat to our children's future health and happiness is widespread. Extinction Rebellion and the broader Climate Emergency Declaration movement also moved the climate conversation forward. I used my training in my environmental science PhD to interpret the science of climate and reach out to climate scientists to piece together simple ways to talk about it with friends and family and my community. My husband and I watched David Attenborough's *Climate Change: The Facts* (2019) together and I felt more able just to be me, to share my fears and hopes more easily with him.

I wrangled parenting, struggled with the usual parenting challenges such as when to get kids to bed, and how long to let them play in the garden, to avoid afternoon and evening tantrums and meltdowns. I wrangled the climate crisis, contemplating ideas for solving it and ways to protect and feed my community in years to come, finding more ways to speak about climate, to meet and connect with others who cared about it, to envisage the world I wanted my children to grow up in. I took my eldest daughter to the school strike in March.

Steve Biddulph, whose writing I greatly respect but I find myself disagreeing with now, tells parents that while standing along side high schoolers at school strikes is important, that taking primary school students to the school strikes may overexpose them to upsetting information. But when I ask my fellow climate parents many of us are taking our young kids to the school strikes and other community based, family friendly climate actions, and they seem, generally, empowered.

I write to Susie Burke from the Australian Psychological Society to find out what she thinks about taking primary school kids to family friendly climate rallies like the school strikes. Her perspective gives me some comfort in regards to my own decisions. Susie believes that participation in these rallies with other family members fosters "active citizen skills" which help them feel capable of making change. Consistent with Susie's experience I have found that making placards with young kids depicting animals and plants that need our protection is not only fun, but gives parents the opportunity to discuss the rally in words and terms that are meaningful to their young children. As Susie has found, going along with other families with young children also helps my kids feel safe and included.

Love leads to action leads to hope

For me, love was how I found my agency. Specifically, love for my children. This agency is the thing we climate activists want everyone to find. Their ability and their bravery to face the facts and then work towards change. I was asked months ago what it is that gives me hope, that makes me optimistic. And it is love that drives me to take action and through that finds hope. Love for my children, and also love for the fascinating and marvellous world we live in. The morning after I hear these words loud and clear in my head I read Mary Heglar's piece 'But the Greatest of These is Love' (2019) where she writes "A love like that … is strong enough, ferocious enough, brave enough" to fight to keep the world okay. And I realised then, too, that morning, that you have to be brave to tackle this crisis. Only the brave can lead. I ponder how to bring along the people that aren't so brave. And I wonder if a little love might help there too. For love is what makes me brave, creative, focused.

But it's the personal that catches up. The moments in between.

My daughter Lucinda threatened to throw my phone away. Because I was, sometimes incessantly, checking and updating *Twitter*, and *Facebook*, at first with my own perspectives and then moderating and sharing content with the groups I am involved with. I learnt that activist burnout is a real issue. I learnt that balancing protecting the future from climate damage with parenting well in the present is quite a juggling act, and a skill set I have to learn and honour.

My children are amazing, wonderful and wilful. They are relatively hard to parent at the best of times. Just this last week though, during my eldest daughter's school holidays, I would say, was a turning point. I inadvertently organised a climate community forum during the Easter holidays. And amidst the stress of this, my daughter's school holiday turned into a rather boring one for her, with a mixture of vacation care and time with me. I was dealing with frustration, and intense emotions bordering on grief and climate anxiety.

I usually try to unpack for myself what the anxious feelings I have are, which ones are climate anxiety, which are from general parenting anxiety and which are personal/life/work anxiety. This helps me manage my emotions. But sometimes, often when life is very busy, or when concerning information becomes public, like the Intergovernmental Panel on Climate Change "Global Warming of 1.5°C" report (IPCC, 2018), all three of these kinds of anxieties can gang up on me at once! In hindsight, my holiday climate forum support would have been a good time to leave the kids with my mum and skip to a café or a park to work on projects, not have my stressed-out countenance anywhere around my kids. I live and learn.

So I committed to making the next school holidays more fun, more relaxed and relatively climate-action free. Switching off as a climate activist is hard. In the world of social media, local and international groups I am part of can have unexpected conversations and concerns arise at any time day and night, and if you don't have some kind of structure, some way to prioritise what is key, to shut off and not feel like you need to be checking in, to know what your role is and what is someone else's, some way to stop, then your daughter wants to throw your phone in the bin and you end up eating microwaved vegetables, potatoes and some form of protein every night.

But I am full of hope. Not just that we will find a way globally to address the climate crisis. But also that I will find a way to strike a better climate-work-life-balance. And for me personally, both these issues are big ones.

I am full of hope, because since I engaged on the climate emergency, it seems millions of children and adults have too. Parenting through the climate crisis asks us to find solutions, to reach out and speak to others, to learn all we can about what is needed so we can help our society and our politicians figure out what needs to be done to give our kids a chance. Using our creativity, our hope, our strategy, our love.

But love also calls us to make sure the now is kind, just as we work to make the future kind. Loving the present requires some self-love too.

And then I realise that to love my kids, to be there for them on their sports days and their under-eights craft days and their numerous children's birthday parties, and to protect their liveable world at the same time, I also need to increase my own 'self-love' or 'self-care.'

Susie Burke acknowledges that for parents, as we engage more deeply with the climate crisis, confronting the reality of what we are up against, continuing to build hope for ourselves and our children can get more difficult, especially as the news of the climate crisis gets steadily worse. But she encourages us to find our own ways to remain hopeful, to persevere on solutions even though they can seem elusive. Climate scientist Kate Marvel (2018) reflects this approach, calling for courage not hope in the face of the climate crisis.

For me, I try to remain brave, which I think sits somewhere between courage and hope — ever since my father, Knox, suggested I remain focused on the solutions. My background in environmental engineering and ecology allows me to engage knowledgeably on the solutions to the climate crisis. I have a fairly unshakable sense that we are going to save a whole lot of this beautiful world for our kids. I let love be my guide, inspired by the very non-climate-related Regina Tomashauser (2003), whose words also helped me finish my pre-climate, pre-kids PhD, and I try to envisage what a beautiful, liveable world will look like for my kids.

Caring for and being in nature can be part of our self-care. Susie Burke reminds me that our determined efforts to safeguard the possibility of a liveable planet will contribute to a better world and give us a sense of purpose and make us feel good. She notes, as I have found, that nature can restore us psychologically, so we should take time out from activism to enjoy revelling in the very nature that we're trying to protect.

To save the future we also have to save the present, to "…love all the things that climate can't change" as film director Josh Fox, who made a film with this phrase in the title, might say (Fox, 2016). We need to be present so we can show the present just how much we love it. To make up the organisational structures and find the helpers so we can disconnect and know when we return to this tricky problem at the end of a glorious weekend when we were switched off, that we can still help solve it.

But taking time out, making space, setting boundaries, this is the skill set I need to work on. I am getting there. I know that I make better decisions when I have had enough sleep. I am letting the adults take responsibility for their own emotions and setting rules and boundaries about how and when I make time to support the forums I moderate, and prioritising the work that I do. I am meeting more and more amazing people who are acting for climate in their small and big ways, who are making me feel that more are sharing the load, and I can take time out to breathe, to recover, to create.

Making the time to share our concerns and knowledge with other adults, when children are not present, Susie Burke believes, is an important part of self-care. On the question of "How careful do we need to be about how we speak about climate change in general around children?" Susie advises parents to be mindful of the presence of young children because in their limited understanding of time and space they may believe the climate threats are imminent and happening to us now.

Finding time for self-care can be hard. But I find ways to care for my kids and myself at once. I find the things that we all love doing, and add more of those to our lives. Like visiting a local butterfly club get together to look at butterflies surrounded by nature next to a playground near Downfall Creek. The look on Lucinda's face as she played with the toy butterflies in our garden after the butterfly club adventure was wonderful. I'm finding the things that my kids love to do that fill up my spirits too. Suddenly the missed under-eights sports day seems less important as the magic of my children acting like butterflies in my garden lifts all our spirits. I am carving the time for the now back into our lives.

I once read a philosophy book that talked about time as a tapestry, not a time-line. So now, as I feel some of my climate action projects starting to flourish and grow through the help of others, I am spending as much time as I can making sure my little girls have as many bright moments, bright days now, and learn to care for nature in ways that light their spirits and give them a sense of power. Because whatever the future holds, I want to know these moments were magical for them. And because I know I make better decisions with more sleep, I also feel strongly that taking time out for these magical moments with my kids is also supporting my activism through making me stronger, more creative and more resilient.

Yes, indeed, I agree that it is critical that I take time out, that I can find ways to step away and nourish my spirits away from this climate fight. That I can slow things down and only take on activities that don't mean my kids have to hear too much of my climate talk. I am not sure how I could have sped up this learning, this discovery, this finding myself on the other side of climate crisis awakening. But I feel like I am on the other side — with school strikers, Fridays for Future, Extinction Rebellion, and all the other little groups like my own Australian Parents for Climate Action who are contributing to raising awareness of the issues, and the urgently required mass mobilisation solutions to address the climate emergency. We are building on and learning more about the work of those who were awake to all this before us, like Pacific Islanders, indigenous leaders in Australia and overseas, and others on the front lines of the climate crisis.

The burden is now being shared by many. The student-led climate strikes in March [and later, in September 2019] were the largest global climate protests ever (Carrington, 2019; Laville, 2019). So we can tag team, we can take time out. We can breathe. Because we are here. And we have found how to speak about the unspeakable. Now we have to make the impossible possible. And we can speak about what we love and want to protect, and how. We can make better decisions, and better connections with people from all walks of life, to talk about the climate crisis, when we are well rested.

Love for nature

Love can help us protect our children's thriving future world in a range of ways. Encouraging love for the natural world is how we can help our children thrive even as it changes. Susie Burke shared with me that it is more important to give our young children opportunities to fall in love with the natural world than to hear us talking about the threats of unmitigated climate change. She encourages me to continue to talk about the environmentally friendly things that I do every day to help my kids learn to appreciate and care for the natural world, and to share my love for it. Lucinda recently made me a picture from stickers of "sea creatures in nature that we are protecting for them" and she is keen to talk to her school about banning glitter at school events to "protect the frogs and the fish" and I find her clear care for our natural world inspiring for me and empowering for her.

Love for climate deniers

And I've found love powerful in another way. By finding ways to love my climate change denying friends. They can help me keep track of the things you sometimes only learn through community, like that it's super critical to turn up to your kids' school sports days and the social niceties that I sometimes lose track of when I am too engaged on the climate crisis. Because, as I learn to advocate for and facilitate solutions to the climate crisis, I am still learning how to parent through it. I haven't been a parent before, this is my first go, and I have to do it through the climate crisis. I need all the help I can get.

Love is here, now

This holiday hasn't been perfect. But Lucinda and I have found our ways to come together. Sometimes when she acts up, a cuddle makes all the difference. I teach her to care for nature, to protect the frogs and the fish. But when I mention climate change sometimes she throws tantrums. So I wonder if she knows more than she needs to. But, even if this is so, she also knows she can march with 10,000 young people and supporters through the streets of Brisbane on climate strike to protect nature, a family friendly action of civic agency Susie Burke says is important to her development. And she knows that I love her and will look after her.

Sometimes I worry whether I have inadvertently said too much in front of my girls about climate change. I try to be careful but sometimes I am sure I slip up. But I like to think that there is a positive sense and comfort that they get from my own knowing I am doing all I can to protect their future. I try to present a calm, caring force for change to my kids and the world. I don't always achieve it but I often do. From what I can see in her sweet, precious, cheeky face, I think Lucinda still thinks I am able to fix things. And I still think I can too, that we can. That we can give the future liveable world a chance to thrive.

Confident, sweet and humorous little Stella believes in me and my efforts to protect her and her world too, I can see this in how she looks at me. But to keep their future safe I need to hold steady in the present. There needs to be less climate chatter in front of my kids, and more frequent walks in nature for our family. I know also that I need more time for rest so I am ready to work to protect my girls' future and their present.

So off to bed I go. My cure for sleepless nights is a gratitude meditation I learnt from a friend. I list five things to myself that I am grateful for each night before bed. Tonight I am thankful for the following:

1 I have my health to be there to help my children find their way through this crisis, and friends, family and community around me should my health ever fail.
2 I have amazing friends who are brave and creative and caring, facing this crisis together.
3 Like on a tapestry, my stitch in time right now is heartbreakingly beautiful. I have beautiful, wild children, perfect Autumn days (in the middle of Winter), views of shimmery water my daughter calls a treat when we drive by…
4 A family that loves me.
5 An unshakable sense we are going to do all we can to protect what we love and give our kids a chance for a thriving, happy, healthy future.

Then I sleep and I dream and I scribble notes in a book. A concept map to save the world. I am always innovating. I am always in love. We have to be the heroes for our time while we care for our littlest heroes.

References

Attenborough, D 2019, *Climate Change: The Facts* [television documentary], BBC Television, London.

Biddulph, S 2013, *Raising Girls*, Finch Publishing, Sydney.

Carrington, D 2019, 'School climate strikes: 1.4 million people took part, say campaigners,' *The Guardian*, 19 March, <https://www.theguardian.com/environment/2019/mar/19/school-climate-strikes-more-than-1-million-took-part-say-campaigners-greta-thunberg>.

Fox, J 2016, *How to Let Go of the World and Love All the Things Climate Can't Change* [documentary film], HBO, New York.

Heglar, M 2019, 'But the Greatest of These is Love,' *medium.com*, <https://medium.com/@maryheglar/but-the-greatest-of-these-is-love-4b7aad06e18c>.

Intergovernmental Panel on Climate Change [IPCC] 2018, *Special Report: Global Warming of 1.5°C*, IPCC, <https://www.ipcc.ch/sr15/>.

Laville, S 2019, 'Across the globe, millions join biggest climate protests ever,' *The Guardian*, 21 September, < https://www.theguardian.com/environment/2019/sep/21/across-the-globe-millions-join-biggest-climate-protest-ever>.

Marvel, K 2018, 'We Need Courage, Not Hope, to Face Climate Change,' *onbeing.org*, <https://onbeing.org/blog/kate-marvel-we-need-courage-not-hope-to-face-climate-change/>.

Tomashauer, R 2003, *Mama Gena's School of Womanly Arts*, Simon & Schuster, New York.

2

Facing the realities of climate change

Susie Burke and Ann Sanson

CLIMATE CHANGE is regarded as one of the most serious global health threats of the twenty-first century (Costello *et al.*, 2009), overall the greatest threat to humanity, and an existential risk to our world (World Economic Forum, 2018). In many parts of the world children's lives are at risk from climate change, and globally they face threats to health and wellbeing. They face a lifetime of coping with climate change, as well as needing to adapt to massive changes in lifestyles as the world transitions to a low-carbon economy. In this essay we discuss how parents can raise children with the skills and attributes to thrive in a climate altered world, as well as cope with their feelings and thoughts about the climate crisis.

Nature of the threat

To avoid warming of more than 1.5°C above pre-industrial times — essential to stabilise the Earth's climate — urgent and strong action all over the globe is required (IPCC, 2018). Scientists "cannot exclude the risk that a cascade of feedbacks could push the 'Earth System' irreversibly onto a 'Hothouse Earth' pathway" (Steffen *et al.*, 2018) which would be catastrophic (IPCC, 2014). It would create a world of unprecedented heatwaves, severe drought, bushfires, flooding and major storms in many regions, with many areas becoming uninhabitable and serious impacts on all human systems and ecosystems. However, our knowledge of the dangers of the climate crisis has not yet led to actions around the world that are commensurate with the threat.

The impacts of climate change on psychological health and wellbeing are varied and complex, but increasingly well documented (Clayton *et al.*, 2017; Hayes *et al.*, 2018). Both the direct and flow-on effects of climate change create physical health impacts ranging from death to illness, while they also place children at risk of mental health consequences including PTSD, depression, anxiety, phobias, sleep disorders, attachment disorders, and substance abuse. These in turn can lead to problems with emotion regulation, cognition, learning, behaviour, language development, and academic performance. Besides negative consequences throughout childhood and adolescence, these also create pre-dispositions to adverse adult mental health outcomes. Further, incremental climate changes such as rising temperatures, rising sea levels, and episodic drought can make large areas uninhabitable, change natural landscapes, disrupt water resources, lessen food production, destroy habitation, weaken infrastructure, force families to leave their homes, and give rise to financial and relationship stresses, all which can impact negatively on children.

Children and young people exhibit high levels of concern over climate change. Even if they have not yet experienced climate change impacts first hand, just knowing about it and the existential threat it poses to their very survival can have a significant psychological impact. Most young people around the world know about it, and many express worry about its impact on their lives. For example, a survey of seven-to-24-year-old Australians found that 96 percent considered climate change to be a serious problem, and 89 percent were worried about its effects. Feelings of disempowerment were significant, and over 70 percent believed that people do not take their opinions on climate change seriously (Chiw & Ling, 2019). Many young people believe that the world may end during their lifetime due to climate change and other global threats (Albert, Hurrelmann, & Quenzel, 2010).

The overarching threats of a changing climate can also give rise to despair and hopelessness as attempts to address this 'wicked problem' seem insignificant in comparison to the scale and magnitude of the threat. Another indication of young people's concerns is the rise of youth social action groups worldwide, such as the School Strikes for Climate which began in Sweden in August 2018, spread to Australia in October, and which have since rapidly spread all around the globe with millions of 'strikers' in thousands of locations in March and September 2019 (Carrington, 2019; Lavill, 2019).

Engaging with the problem of climate change — parents' responsibilities

How to help children to cope with their feelings and thoughts about climate change, as well as preparing them to cope with and adapt to its ongoing impacts and the chaos they may encounter during a rapid transition to a zero carbon world, is becoming of increasing interest to psychologists, educators, and of course, parents. Whilst parents face many challenges in their efforts to provide their children with the best possible opportunities for their future health, happiness, and success, climate change is perhaps the most wide-ranging, pervasive, and certain of the longer-term threats that they need to consider.

Social scientists have spent many years researching how people think about and understand climate change and other environmental threats, how they cope with and come to terms with them, and the barriers that can get in the way of doing something effective about it. This research is of course very relevant to a discussion about how parents can support their children, because in order to communicate with children about climate change, parents also need to overcome their own tendencies to minimise and avoid the issue.

Scientists have found that, although most people accept that anthropogenic climate change is a serious problem and that urgent changes are needed, many avoid thinking about it or changing their behaviour (Marshall, 2014). There are numerous psychological factors which contribute to avoidance, minimisation and denial, including the tendency to see climate change as distant in time and space, hence not needing personal and urgent attention (Uzzell, 2000); becoming desensitised to the problem and mentally tuning out (O'Neill & Nicholson-Cole, 2009); ideological resistance because proposed solutions seem to threaten the 'system' they are familiar with or values they hold dear (Feygina, Jost & Goldsmith, 2010); and a desire to avoid distressing feelings aroused by thinking about it (Norgaard, 2011; see Marshall, 2014, for a summary). Being aware of these cognitive biases is an important first step in overcoming them. The *Climate Change Empowerment Handbook* (APS, 2018a) offers eight strategies (which together make the acronym ACTIVATE) to help people deal with these social and psychological obstacles.

Many of these cognitive biases can be in play with parents. In fact, Marshall (2014) suggests that parents may be even more inclined to employ the full range of biases and avoidance strategies. "Having children is usually an active choice in which we quite deliberately choose to highlight the reasons for having the child and suppress our knowledge about the world we might be bringing them into. Presuming that we wish the best for our children … this inclines us to an optimism bias concerning climate change and certainly concerning the prospects for our own children." (Marshall, 2014, p. 189)

Philosopher Elizabeth Cripps (2017) argues, however, that parents have a moral responsibility to protect their children's interests and that current parents may be the only generation who can act to mitigate climate change and adequately protect their further descendants' basic interests. Cripps thus focuses on parents' duty to act to mitigate climate change. While we agree wholeheartedly with her argument, as psychologists our interest is also in how parents can help children to cope and thrive in a climate altered world. This is our focus in the rest of this essay. We argue that raising children in a climate changed world requires three major tasks, in addition to parents' own activities to mitigate its severity: imparting pro-environmental values, communicating effectively and helpfully about climate change, and helping them to cope, by building their skills and capacities to engage in both climate change mitigation (i.e., taking action to reduce the severity of climate change) and climate change adaptation (i.e., preparing for its effects).

Imparting pro-environmental values

Studies show that parents can play an important role in transmitting knowledge, competencies and a pro-environmental orientation to their children throughout their childhood and adolescence (Matthies & Wallis, 2015). They show that learning rather than maturation is important here. Through social influence processes, parents help build their children's and teenagers' environmentally related values, attitudes and behaviour. Despite the increasing influence of peers and other societal agents in these years, parental behaviour, family norms, and communication still exert a significant influence on young people's pro-environmentalism (Matthies & Wallis, 2015). Across cultures, the home is an important site for developing environmentally engaged children (Gonhoj & Thogersen, 2017).

Researchers have found that there are three phases in developing human-nature connections: Being *in* nature, being *with* nature, and being *for* nature (Giusti et al., 2018). In other words, before feeling care or concern for the environment, and before feeling responsible and motivated to act to protect it, a child has to at least feel at ease and comfortable in the natural elements of the outdoors. Parents can look for environments that allow their children to build a nature connection — these are environments which have a number of qualities, like 'entertainment', 'awe', 'engagement of senses', 'surprise', 'physical activity', and others.

Talking with children about climate change

Parents are often tempted to try to shield their children from the facts about climate change. But this is not possible, given widespread media coverage — and most already know about it. Nor is it fair, since children have a right to know about the things that threaten their lives, and to have a voice and be involved in protecting themselves (United Nations General Assembly, 1989).

How we talk with children depends on their age, and their interests, engagement, and language skills. Children are at different places in their knowledge and concern, and many are already much more knowledgeable and engaged than the adults around them.

Whilst conversations with younger children tend to focus on helping them "fall in love with nature," it is important that parents don't underestimate their interest in the state of the earth, and their personal competencies (Engdahl, 2015). Parents are encouraged to use reflective listening skills, to draw out children's ideas, and empower them to get involved in everyday things they can do together to keep the natural world healthy, like planting trees, mending things rather than throwing them away, and composting. Conversations about climate change at this age also often involve talking about extreme weather events like bushfires, floods, and cyclones.

For children living in vulnerable places, these conversations include practical and psychological preparedness activities (see APS disaster resources: https://www.psychology.org.au/for-the-public/Psychology-topics/Disasters/Preparing-for-disasters). In the aftermath of disasters, these conversations might include helping children to find ways of expressing their feelings, reassuring them that they are safe, and looking out for the numerous helpers who rise up to help make our world better.

In late childhood and adolescence, parents can extend their ways of talking to children about climate change, as they begin to think in more abstract ways. They are then more capable of viewing climate change as not just extreme weather events but as a multi-faceted global challenge involving long-term changes and complex feedback loops (Chawla & Flanders Cushing, 2007).

For some children and young people, parental conversations are key for helping them develop an awareness of climate change. For example, Stevenson, Peterson, and Bondell (2016) found that climate change concern among U.S. adolescents was predicted both by frequency of discussion with parents about climate change and parents' acceptance of its reality. In other families, children are already more knowledgeable than their parents (as they often are about technology and social media also!). Children are engaged with climate problems, are distressed by the current and predicted impacts, and are angry about inaction. For them, parents' roles include acknowledging the validity of their children's thoughts and feelings, clarifying their understanding if needed, and helping them build courage and hope through shared action. We look at all these ways of helping children to cope with the reality of climate change in more detail in the following section.

Helping children to cope

Coping with climate change is about being able to deal effectively with the distress of climate change — not just dealing with extreme weather disasters, but also being able to deal with the existential and vicarious distress being felt by many young people around the world, and then staying engaged with the problem. Environmental psychologists often use the term 'psychological adaptation' to talk about how children are 'coming to terms' with the climate crisis. Coping, or psychological adaptation, means making sense of climate change, managing the associated feelings, and engaging with the problem. Three types of coping have been identified in research, each of which can be helpful: emotion-focused coping, meaning-focused coping, and problem-focused coping.

Helping children deal with feelings about climate change — emotion-focused coping

Social scientists use the term emotion-focused coping to talk about the things that we do to cope with upsetting feelings. How people respond to distressing feelings about climate change is very important. People can react in very unhelpful ways, e.g., by trying to minimise the threat, or endlessly distracting themselves, or feeling helpless and resigned to the disaster (APS, 2018a). A more useful response is to acknowledge and manage these feelings so that we stay engaged and do not just try to push them away, or get overwhelmed. We call this skill emotion regulation. People can help children to cope with feelings by helping them to put words to their emotions, validating them, saying things like "it makes sense that you're feeling sad about the coral dying" and "I can understand that you feel angry with adults for not acting on the problem"; and practicing calming techniques with them like slow breathing (e.g. "breathe like a lazy dog sleeping in the sunshine"), and self-talk (e.g. "I'm ok"; "I can handle this").

Cultivating hope — meaning-focused coping

Another technique for coping with climate change is to cultivate ways of thinking about the problem which build hope. A Swedish environmental psychologist who studies children's coping with climate change, Maria Ojala, calls this 'meaning-focused coping.' It involves positive reappraisal, where we teach children to look at the problem in a different way, like focusing on how healthy our world will be as we transition to green power, ride more (and drive less), eat less red meat, and share more resources with our neighbours, and so on.

Another strategy is to help children focus on all the millions of people who are also working on solutions. Building optimism and realistic hope is especially important when a problem cannot be removed or solved immediately, but demands active involvement over the longer term. Parents can show their children how they developed their own strong 'inner strength muscles' to keep going even when things seem daunting and hopeless, by taking action to make the planet safe (e.g. "There's always a difference to be made." See APS Tip Sheets (APS, 2018b and c) for more examples.

Helping children to take action — Problem-focused coping

It feels good to have a purpose and to work for a better world — action is an antidote to despair and anxiety. Problem-focused coping involves treating children as agents in solving the problem of climate change, not just as victims, and involves efforts to reduce the cause of the problem that is creating stress. It is an excellent strategy being used by children all around the world to protect the environment. Actions can range from things young people can do in their own homes, school and communities, right up to the political level.

The School Strike for Climate movement is one example of children taking action to demand good climate policy from leaders, and which shows how working together with others can have a greater impact — and be fun! In Colombia, a child-led court action has recently resulted in the government being required to protect children's future environment, and protect the Amazon rainforest in its own right (Our Children's Trust, 2018). Similar court cases are underway in many parts of the world. Children around the world are also actively engaging in practical mitigation and adaptation actions, like promoting the use of renewable energy, tree and mangrove planting, and petitioning successfully to have their school moved from the path of potential future landslides in the Philippines (e.g. Plan International, 2015).

Skills and attributes for children to thrive in a changed world

Children are going to be living in a climate-altered world even with swift action on climate change, and many parents are concerned about how to help prepare them to live happy, productive and engaged lives in a rapidly changing world and more extreme climate.

Climate change is likely to create conditions such as resource shortages, increased inequality, and major migrations which can easily erupt in conflict and violence, so skills and attributes such as conflict resolution, empathy and acceptance, and beliefs in equality and justice will be critical in the next generation. A low-carbon economy, essential as we drastically reduce emissions, is likely to involve more interconnected communities relying on localised food and energy sources, reducing energy costs in travel/transport, and sharing more resources. To thrive in this scenario, skills for cooperation and shared action, and strong community orientation and engagement will be helpful. Helping young people to develop all these skills and attributes is therefore important.

These skills and attributes will not only be critically important to a climate altered world, they are also key to the healthy positive development of young people in general. Psychologists who research positive development have shown that there are four broad factors from childhood through early adolescence which help build them: self-regulation; positive and supportive relationships with parents, peers, and teachers; school connectedness; and being a contributing member of their community, including volunteering and political awareness (Hawkins, *et al.*, 2009). Helping to foster these factors early in life is thus of critical importance.

Self-regulation is a term that psychologists use to describe skills that children learn to be able to monitor their own behaviour, thoughts, feelings, and to manage these so as to behave in pro-social ways that are in line with their highest values. Self-regulation includes things like being able to calm down when upset, delay gratification, and pick yourself up again when feeling low or sad. These are the skills that we covered in the section above on emotion-focused coping. Parents can help build them by valuing these emotional intelligence skills at least as much as academic skills.

Positive and supportive relationships can be promoted by fostering a range of interpersonal skills like cooperation, turn taking, learning how to 'work it out' with a friend when a problem arises rather than just quitting or fighting, learning how to be a 'giver,' sharing and cooperation, and learning negotiation and conflict resolution skills. Parents can foster these by being interested in their children's friends, and learning and using negotiation skills themselves when dealing with conflict with their children. Trying to make sure that your child feels a sense of belonging and connection at school is also a key factor, encouraging them to develop good relationships with teachers and classmates, and parents themselves engaging with the school to solve problems.

Finally, skills of social engagement (helping children to make a difference in their communities) and civic engagement (helping them to become good citizens in the world) are also critically important skills for positive development and thriving in a climate altered world. To solve climate change and live in a climate-altered world, people need to be closely connected with their communities (e.g. to share resources and rebuild after climate shocks) and actively supportive of strong climate policies. Encouraging children to engage meaningfully with neighbours, volunteer in community events, learn how to speak out about problems that concern them, and recognise their own ability to make a difference can help build these skills. Many children are already very aware of bigger-than-self issues, and helping them to turn these concerns into action is a very useful way that parents can help.

To sum up, children need our best thinking to ensure they grow up happy and healthy, and today our best thinking needs to acknowledge the terrifying reality of climate change, and the threat that it poses to our children's very existence. As Cripps points out, we are most likely the last generation with the chance to protect our descendants' interests. Amidst all of the other challenges of parenting, acting to mitigate climate change, raising children to fall in love with nature so that they become protectors of nature, and preparing them for a climate altered world have become critical responsibilities.

Beyond all this, we also need to help our children, and ourselves, to build the courage to face the frightening realities of climate change (despite the uncertainty of success), but to choose anyway to act with moral integrity and hope, because doing nothing is not an option. The future is unknown, which means it is open to the imagination and always possible to influence in some way. Paul Gilding, former Greenpeace director, reminds us that, if the human species specialises in one thing, it's taking on the impossible: "Do something extraordinary. It's what humans do." (Gilding, 2018)

References

Albert, M, Hurrelmann, K & Quenzel, G 2010, 'Youth 2010: Self-assertion despite uncertainty?', in Albert, M, Hurrelmann, K, & Quenzel, G (eds), *Youth 2010, Shell Youth Study 16*, Fischer-Taschenbuch-Verl., Frankfurt, Germany, pp. 37-51.

Australian Psychological Society [APS] 2018a, *The climate change empowerment handbook*, The Australian Psychological Society, Melbourne, <https://www.psychology.org.au/getmedia/88ee1716-2604-44ce-b87a-ca0408dfaa12/Climate-change-empowerment-handbook.pdf>.

Australian Psychological Society [APS] 2018b, *A guide for parents about the climate crisis*, The Australian Psychological Society, Melbourne, <https://www.psychology.org.au/for-the-public/Psychology-topics/Climate-change-psychology/Talking-with-children-about-the-environment/A-guide-for-parents-about-the-climate-crisis>.

Australian Psychological Society [APS] 2018c, R*aising children to thrive in a climate changed world*, The Australian Psychological Society, Melbourne, <https://www.psychology.org.au/for-the-public/Psychology-topics/Climate-change-psychology/Talking-with-children-about-the-environment/Raising-children-to-thrive-in-a-climate-changed-wo>.

Carrington, D 2019, 'School climate strikes: 1.4 million people took part, say campaigners,' *The Guardian*, 19 March, <https://www.theguardian.com/environment/2019/mar/19/school-climate-strikes-more-than-1-million-took-part-say-campaigners-greta-thunberg>.

Chawla, L & Flanders Cushing, D 2007, 'Education for strategic environmental behaviour,' *Environmental Education Research*, vol. 13, no. 4, pp. 437–452.

Chiw, A & Ling, H 2019, Young people of Australia and climate change: *Perceptions and concerns. A report for millennium kids*, millenniumkids.com, <https://www.millenniumkids.com.au/wp-content/uploads/2019/02/Young-People-and-Climate-Change.pdf>.

Clayton, S, Manning, C, Krygsman & K, Speiser, M 2017, Mental health and our changing climate: Impacts, implications, and guidance, American Psychological Association, and ecoAmerica, Washington, DC.

Costello, A, Abbas, M *et al.* 2009, 'Managing the health effects of climate change,' *The Lancet*, vol. 373 (9676), pp. 1693-1708.

Cripps, E 2017, 'Do parents have a special duty to mitigate climate change?,' *Politics, Philosophy & Economics*, vol. 16, no. 3, pp. 308–325.

Engdahl, I 2015, 'Early childhood education for sustainability: The OMEP world project,' *International Journal of Early Childhood*, vol. 47, no. 3, pp. 347–366.

Feygina, I, Jost, J T & Goldsmith, R E 2010, 'System justification, the denial of global warming, and the possibility of "system- sanctioned change,"' *Personality and Social Psychology Bulletin*, vol. 36, no. 3, pp. 326–338.

Gilding, P 2018, *Climate change as a global emergency*, Darebin Climate Emergency Conference, <https://climateemergencydeclaration.org/darebin-climate-emergency-conference-see-the-presentations/>.

Giusti, M, Svane, U, Raymond, C & Beery, T 2018, 'A Framework to Assess Where and How Children Connect to Nature,' *Frontiers in Psychology*, vol. 8, pp. 2283. [online]

Gronhoj, A & Thogersen, J 2017, 'Why young people do things for the environment: The role of parenting for adolescents' motivation to engage in pro-environmental behaviour,' *Journal of Environmental Psychology*, vol. 54, pp. 11-19.

Hawkins, M T, Letcher P, Sanson A, *et al* 2009, 'Positive development in emerging adulthood,' *Australian Journal of Psychology*, vol. 61, no. 2, pp. 89-99.

Hayes, K, Blashki, G, Wiseman, J, Burke, S, *et al* 2018, 'Climate change and mental health: risks, impacts and priority actions,' *Journal of Mental Health Systems*, vol. 12, no. 1, pp. 1-12.

Intergovernmental Panel on Climate Change [IPCC] 2014, *Climate Change 2014: Synthesis Report. Contribution of Working Groups I, II and III to the Fifth Assessment Report of the Intergovernmental Panel on Climate Change*, IPCC, Geneva, Switzerland.

Intergovernmental Panel on Climate Change [IPCC] 2018, *Special Report: Global Warming of 1.5°C*, IPCC, <https://www.ipcc.ch/sr15/>.

Laville, S 2019, 'Across the globe, millions join biggest climate protests ever,' *The Guardian*, 21 September, <https://www.theguardian.com/environment/2019/sep/21/across-the-globe-millions-join-biggest-climate-protest-ever>.

Marshall, G 2014, *Don't even think about it. Why our brains are wired to ignore climate change*, Bloomsbury Press, London.

Matthies, E & Wallis, H 2015, 'Family socialization and sustainable consumption,' in Reisch, L & Thøgersen, J (eds), *Handbook of Research on Sustainable Consumption*, Edward Elgar Publishing, Cheltenham, Northampton, pp. 268- 284.

Norgaard, K 2011, *Living in denial: Climate change, emotions, and everyday life*, MIT Press, Cambridge Mass.

Ojala, M 2012, 'Regulating worry, promoting hope: How do children, adolescents and young adults cope psychologically with climate change?' *International Journal of Environmental Science Education*, vol. 7, no. 4, pp. 537-561.

Ojala, M 2013, 'Coping with climate change among adolescents: Implications for subjective well-being and environmental engagement,' *Sustainability*, vol. 5, no. 5, pp. 2191-2209.

O'Neill, S & Nicholson-Cole, S 2009, ' "Fear won't do it": Promoting positive engagement with climate change through visual and iconic representations,' *Science Communication*, vol. 30, no. 3, pp. 355-379.

Our Children's Trust 2018, *Columbia*, Our Children's Trust, <https://www.ourchildrenstrust.org/colombia>.

Plan International 2015, *We stand as one: Children, young people and climate change*, Plan International, <https://www.plan.org.au/-/media/plan/documents/resources/we-stand-as-one--children-young-people-and-climate-change.pdf>.

Steffen, W, Rockström, J, Richardson, *et al* 2018, Trajectories of the Earth System in the Anthropocene, *Proceedings of the National Academy of Sciences of the United States of*

America, vol. 115, no. 33, pp. 8252-8259.

Stevenson, K, Peterson, M & Bondell, H 2016, 'The influence of personal beliefs, friends, and family in building climate change concern among adolescents,' *Journal of Environmental Education Research*, 2016 [online], pp. 1-14.

Spratt, D & Dunlop, I 2019, *Existential climate-related security risk: A scenario approach*, Breakthrough: National Centre for Climate Restoration, Melbourne, <https://docs.wixstatic.com/ugd/148cb0_a1406e0143ac4c469196d3003bc1e687.pdf>.

Strife, S 2012, 'Children's environmental concerns: Expressing ecophobia,' *Journal of Environmental Education*, vol. 43, no. 1, pp. 37-54.

United Nations General Assembly 1989, *Convention on the Rights of the Child* [Treaty Series No. 1577], United Nations, New York, <http://www.refworld.org/docid/3ae6b38f0.html>.

UNICEF [United Nations Children's Fund] 2014, *The challenges of climate change: children on the front line*, Innocenti Insight: UNICEF Office of Research, Florence, Italy, <https://www.unicef-irc.org/publications/series/insights/>.

Uzzell, D 2000, 'The Psycho-Spatial dimension of global environmental problems,' *Journal of Environmental Psychology*, vol. 20, no. 4, pp. 307–318.

World Economic Forum 2018, *The Global Risks Report 2018, 13th Edition*, The World Economic Forum, Geneva, Switzerland, <https://www.weforum.org/reports/the-global-risks-report-2018>.

Developing climate consciousness
7 Ways in 7 Days

Rachel Forgasz

TO RAISE CHILDREN who will survive the climate crisis we will need to teach them much more than the facts about carbon emissions. Our calamitously hothouse earth is just a symptom of the much deeper crisis humanity must face: a crisis of conscience and of consciousness. For tomorrow's generations to survive it, we must reassess today's social, political, and economic systems and rethink every aspect of our lives through the lens of a new sensibility that I call climate consciousness. And we need to do it fast.

When I started work on *7 Ways in 7 Days* at the end of 2018, I was developing it as a simple framework for adults to use to support children to develop climate consciousness. My plan for this essay was to provide a range of practical illustrations of how you as parents might use *7 Ways in 7 Days* to nurture the climate consciousness of children at different developmental stages and in a range of contexts.

However, as I witnessed the explosive rise of global youth climate activism, I began to suspect that the greatest obstacle to evolving the consciousness of children was, in fact, us: the adults who teach them tacit and explicit lessons about how to be human. This was confirmed beyond doubt when the Australian people re-elected a conservative, coal-loving, climate-change-denying government in May 2019. Even in the best cases, and despite all our efforts, many of us do not (yet) embody the consciousness we hope to nurture in children and are unwittingly instilling the same ways of being that have initiated the sixth mass extinction of life on earth.

Perhaps this is why I decided to write expansively about the *7 Ways* themselves, explicitly unpacking my thinking about how each one supports the transition to climate consciousness before providing suggestions for implementing *7 Ways in 7 Days.* These are designed to encourage the transformational learning of parents and children side by side. I have made a point of including some suggestions for supporting the learning of very young children in particular, and for including extended family and school communities. Somewhere in all of this, I hope you will find something of value.

Climate consciousness: How on earth will we get there?

I work as an academic in a university faculty of education where I teach people how to teach. I research and write about teaching that encourages deep learning and the things that prevent it. I am particularly interested in the complex influence of emotion on learning. For example, let's think about how a learner's feelings of safety, of comfort and discomfort, might impact their learning. On one hand, we can think about the vulnerability of being a learner, the risk that you will feel humiliated or ashamed for asking a stupid question or giving the wrong answer.

These fears are an inhibiting force that can prevent learning, so it is important that we create safe learning spaces in which there are no stupid questions and it is comfortable to try and fail. On the other hand, there is the familiar refrain that if you are looking for improvement and growth, you will find it just outside your comfort zone. We say that comfort breeds complacency, that until you experience discomfort, you feel no impetus for change.

Deep, transformational learning is only possible in the elusive space between safety and challenge, where learners feel able to remain comfortably uncomfortable. Climate scientists and activists have been grappling with this for decades. How to generate enough discomfort about climate change to snap us out of our comfortably-comfortable complacency and catalyse our desire for change, without provoking so much discomfort that we end up feeling too scared or too ashamed to act. How to make us comfortably uncomfortable.

At this point, some of you might feel like shouting at me to get over myself, that the end of the world isn't going to wait around for us to get comfortable with our discomfort. That the governments of the world must take immediate emergency action and enforce the necessary changes that we are too uncomfortable to face. But while changing the rules will undoubtedly change our actions, there is a limit to what we can achieve through behaviour change alone. If our attitudes, values, and beliefs remain the same, nothing really changes at all.

It is extremely difficult to shift our beliefs, especially the core beliefs we have held since childhood and which do not occur to us as beliefs at all but as truths. The consequences of embracing change at this level are so disorienting, so uncomfortably uncomfortable, that people are more likely to cling instead to irrational beliefs and unconscionable actions.

If we are to save ourselves and our planet, we must be willing to reconsider our dearest held values and our deepest held beliefs about ourselves and the world. Am I a good person? What do I want? What state is the world in? Am I successful? Am I safe? Will anyone protect me if I am not? Confronting such questions is only really possible if we feel comfortably uncomfortable about engaging with ourselves and one another at the very deepest level.

How to get comfortably uncomfortable:
7 Ways in 7 Days

7 Ways in 7 Days supports our transition to climate consciousness by breaking down the process into seven bite sized pieces, one for each day of the week.

Focus on the development of just one aspect of climate consciousness each day. This reduces our risk of feeling overwhelmed and supports us to maintain an attitude of comfortable discomfort when responding to the challenges we will inevitably have to confront about our attitudes and ourselves. With everyone focused on the same *Way* each day, it will be easier to support each other's individual development and to grow into new ways of being together as a family.

Focus on the same aspect on the same day each week. This is a common approach to managing the instability of change by encouraging the development of new routines and habits. Over time, daily actions and attitudes that were once impossibly uncomfortable will feel more and more comfortable until they are easy to adopt across the board. Notice if you start to feel comfortably comfortable. Push your limits. Aim to remain on the learning edge of comfortable discomfort.

Develop rituals. As you repeat its weekly cycle, you might find that some rituals are developing organically around your *7 Ways* practice. One of the original motivations for *7 Ways in 7 Days* was my own need to connect with friends and family to support our transition to climate consciousness. I imagined all kinds of rituals for connecting over each day's way. Even the simple ritual of sharing *7 Ways* stories over dinner can bolster your sense commitment and give your individual actions a sense of collective significance. I have included a few examples of the diverse ways we might think about 'ritual' in the context of contemporary and secular family life. You are welcome to try them but I really encourage you to invent your own.

Day 1
Reduce your impact
Meat-free Monday

It is unreasonable to expect consumers to shoulder responsibility for climate change. It is also unrealistic to imagine that our consumer choices alone make any meaningful difference. Nevertheless, our planet's finite resources are fast running out and the affluent West has already consumed much more than its fair share. Simply put: we must reduce our impact by cutting our consumption of Earth's energy and resources.

The combined impacts of industrialised agriculture produce more emissions than the entire global transport industry. It is also the chief cause of wildlife extinction through habitat loss. A sustainable food industry for people and planet hinges on reducing global meat consumption by 50 percent overall and up to 90 percent in affluent Western countries such as Australia (deeplygoodmag, 2019). Adopting a plant-based diet has been identified as the most significant positive difference that individuals can make in response to our climate crisis (Carrington, 2018). It is also one of the most contentious. Why is that?

In many cultures, food is the centre of family life. Food has weighty symbolic significance, too. For my grandparents' generation, meat was a sign of abundance, of plenty. Its absence invoked memories of wartime rationing or else the shame of their poverty as migrants. Today, the availability of meat is so taken for granted that many of us simply don't know what or how to cook without it. And if you are someone who already cooks out of a sense of parental responsibility (as opposed to culinary delight), being asked to cater for vegetarians adds yet another layer of burden. All this may well be true but what is perhaps more significant is that when children say, "I read that we should eat less meat," what many parents hear is, "you're a bad person." Notice when any resistance arises in conversations like these — in yourself or in others. Take the resistance as a sign of discomfort and support the way back to a safe space for learning.

If you are a meat-eating household, committing to *Meat-free Monday* is a great way to ease your family's transition to a more sustainable diet. If you are already vegetarian, eat vegan. If you're vegan, invite non-vegan friends and family to dinner.

On *Meat-free Monday*, try to cook only with what is in-season and with locally sourced, organic produce. Actively involve kids in every aspect from selecting the recipe to cooking the meal. (Re)learn together what it means to eat a nutrient-rich and balanced diet that contributes to the good health of both people and planet.

Day 2
Question convenience
Transport Tuesday

Many of our daily choices are determined by convenience: how to travel (whatever is quickest), what to eat (whatever is easiest), and what to buy (whatever is cheapest). When we prioritise convenience, we are privileging what is personally best for us in the short term with little concern about the long term impact of our choices on our own bodies and psyches, let alone on other people from far away parts of the planet. Convenience is a kind of self-concern. As a rationale for decision-making, it is the opposite of ethics and the opposite of care. Not the sort of *attitude* we intend to nurture in children but one that we tacitly reinforce through their daily experiences.

Developing climate consciousness requires willingness to question both the concept and the consequences of convenience from an ethical perspective. Convenient for whom? Convenient at what price? And at whose expense? It means caring about the answers and making different choices accordingly. You might be thinking, "I can't afford to do that," but when you question the true cost of convenience, you see that, in truth, you really can't afford not to.

For example, I am guessing that many of you would have dismissed my *Meat-free Monday* suggestion to cook with local, organic produce as being too expensive, too difficult, or too time consuming. Too inconvenient, in other words, for working parents to seriously consider. But what are the *true costs* of the convenient alternatives?

Let's start with *nonorganic* agricultural practices. In theory, the use of pesticides is supposed to improve the cost and efficiency of our food supply by protecting crops from damage by pests. In reality, pesticides quickly degrade the fertility and drought-resistance of soils which means less growth and greater expense. Pesticides also contaminate water supplies on the ground and devastate surrounding bee and insect populations when airborne (Pariona, 2017).

Then there are the environmental costs of *importing* produce. These include the greenhouse gases emitted to transport it and to refrigerate it before, during and after transit, additional consumption of energy and resources to manufacture protective transit packaging that often ends up in landfill, and the further release of methane when excess and spoiled produce gets sent to landfill too (Sonesson, Davis & Ziegler, 2009). Meanwhile, the *nutritional quality* of 'fresh' supermarket produce is further compromised with the use of chemical fungicides to prevent mould while vitamin levels simultaneously decline as a consequence of cold storage over time (Clemons, 2014).

Convenience at *what* price? At *whose* expense?

Transport Tuesday is an invitation to practise making ethical choices even if they are inconvenient. Here's how: wherever you are going, prioritise sustainability when deciding how you will get there. This might mean taking public transport, carpooling, walking, or riding a bike. If you have school-aged children, you might ask the school to support a weekly carpooling initiative for parents or a walk-or-ride-to-school campaign. If, for whatever reason, transport change isn't an option for you, choose another area of daily decision making as the focus of your weekly commitment to question convenience.

As a family, reassess all your consumer choices — from food to fashion, personal hygiene, and household cleaning products — from an ethical perspective. Question the priorities that drive your choices. Consider the buy-now-pay-later costs and the here-and-there consequences for animals, plants, and planet. Having questioned convenience as an *attitude* and decided to care about its costs, you may find yourself making radically different choices, not because you feel you have to, but because it is what you want.

Day 3
Get informed
Watch-it Wednesday

The extent of our climate emergency has been concealed from us for decades through euphemisms, fake news, and deliberate acts of duplicity perpetrated by governments and corporations. Coming to terms with this is terrifying and it raises all kinds of agonising questions about what we can believe and who we can trust. Equally excruciating is the acknowledgement that, for far too long, we have been the willing accomplices to our own deception. There is certainly no shortage of information out there so why don't we want to get ourselves informed?

For one thing, ignorance is *comfortably comfortable bliss*. Besides, with so much information out there, even trying to decide where to start feels *uncomfortably uncomfortable* to the point of paralysis. And even though knowledge is power, it comes with the responsibility to act as though we know what we know, and that means residing in a perpetual state of *comfortable discomfort*. The thing is, we already know far too much so pretending not to know will only ever allow us feel *uncomfortably comfortable* at best.

Maintaining the pretence in order to 'protect' children from painful truths about our planet is not only exhausting, it is isolating for everyone and is much more likely to *contribute* to children's eco-anxiety in the long term as their unexpressed fears and feelings mount up over time (Fawbert, 2019). On the other hand, encouraging children's learning about the problems of climate crisis is important in building the resilience they will need to face the future (Weston, 2019). Exploring how to take action on climate crisis can empower children by alleviating the sense of helplessness that often accompanies their eco-anxiety (Fawbert, 2019). And there is an enormous range of quality resources available to support climate conversations with children. All you have to do is decide to want to find them.

Beyond the immediate matter of getting informed about climate, it is also important to consider the bigger picture implications of our choices in terms of the *attitudes* we are modelling and tacitly condoning. As an attitude, 'wanting to know' supports the capacity to be responsible, curious, and empathetic. An attitude of 'not wanting to know' encourages apathy, denial, and withholding.

Every *Watch-it Wednesday* is an opportunity to adopt an attitude of 'wanting to know' and reaffirm your commitment to get informed. The premise is simple: as a family, choose a climate-related topic you want to learn about and find something to watch (or read) to get you started. How deep you go is up to you and may vary from week to week. It could be anything from watching an online video while you do the dishes to hosting a feature length documentary screening for your extended family and friends. You can use *Watch-it Wednesdays* to follow up on questions and conversations that come up about the other *Ways*. And remember, getting informed needn't be grim. Celebrating the beauty of the natural world, getting inspired by other climate activists, and learning techniques for vegan chocolate-making are just a few joyous alternatives.

Day 4
Quit consumerism
Thank-you Thursday

Having already covered the need to reduce your impact (Monday) and question convenience (Tuesday), you would be forgiven for wondering if these *7 Ways* are getting a bit repetitious. But while the outcomes might appear similar, it is the motivation for change that most significantly distinguishes one way from the others. Monday invites the simple *behavioural change* of reducing our resource consumption. Tuesday encourages the *attitudinal change* of prioritising the ethics of our choices over the personal cost. Thursday acknowledges that although we might be willing to commit to making these changes, most of us will probably think of them as 'sacrifices' until our fundamental *beliefs* about material things are thrown into question.

Things are the markers of identity. Our things tell the world who we are. The more money we have, the more things we can have, the more 'whos' we can choose to be. Our things also tell us how much we are worth. The more we have, the more we are, the more we want to be. To be more, we need more. The more we feed the need for more, the more we need, the more we feed. And since we are nothing without our stuff, we will never *have* enough and we will never *be* enough but we will keep on trying to fill the void with more and more stuff. Our insatiable appetites demanding to be fed, we will ravage Earth's resources until we eat ourselves to death.

Even if you can't see it yet, if you live in a consumer capitalist society, it is important to at least contemplate the *possibility* that this somehow gets to the ugly heart of your core beliefs about yourself and your relationship with things. And if you have children, to consider the subtle and not so subtle ways in which they might be taking on those beliefs too. Every *Thank-you Thursday* is an invitation to return to that contemplation. It is also an opportunity to explore another way of being and seeing ourselves in the world. Because while we might have the willpower to modify some of our consumer behaviours, we will only truly quit consumerism when we find another way to feed our very natural hunger to be felt and seen. On *Thank-you Thursday*, we practise the possibility of filling up on the experience and expression of gratitude.

You can cultivate gratitude among young kids with a morning ritual in which they each honour their favourite toy of the moment and then swap toys for the day to nurture a sharing mindset. Dissociating kids' sense of themselves from their stuff is a significant way to disrupt their blind adoption of consumerist beliefs. End *Thank-you Thursdays* with a simple dinner-time ritual in which you each share a moment of gratitude from the day or week just passed. If your stories are about other people, send a message to let them know and extend your circle of thanks.

You can also use *Thank-you Thursdays* as a training ground to tackle your consumer tendencies head on. If you find you need to buy something, choose not to. Make do with what you have, give thanks, and fill up on the satisfaction of your own resourcefulness. In time, with an attitude of gratitude, we may start to believe that we do have enough. We are enough. And no longer hungry for more.

Day 5
Connect
Feeling-it Friday

Many of us have been taught to value reason over emotion and to dismiss, judge, and manage our feelings. But left unacknowledged, it is far more likely that our feelings are managing us, the unconscious drivers of our actions, attitudes, and beliefs. Chief amongst them is fear.

In an evolutionary sense, fear is vital. It is the mechanism that makes us alert and responsive to the threat of potential harm. In the concrete jungle of consumer culture, it's survival of the biggest, the newest, and best. We buy product after product, each one promising the security of belonging and the safety of strong self-concept and self-worth. We chase an endless stream of impossible ideals in the constant fear that no matter what we have, we will always need more.

This fear makes us mis-recognise our abundance as scarcity so that we feel perfectly justified in choosing convenience and cost-effectiveness over the consequences. We can close our eyes to factory farming, turn our backs on child slave labour, and shut our ears to cries of climate crisis because we genuinely *believe* that we cannot afford to care.

Because our fears turn our attention inward on ourselves, we have no real capacity to empathise, to care, or connect. This lack of connection among young people has been evident over recent years in reports of declining feelings of belonging among Australian school-aged children (McGowan, 2018), the growing incidence of celibacy syndrome among young Japanese adults (Haworth, 2013), and an epidemic of youth loneliness in the UK (Monbiot, 2014). Social disconnection is easily exacerbated by online engagement in virtual spaces where there is also a separation of our thinking selves from our feeling bodies and the natural world.

Feeling-it Friday is an invitation to connect with our disconnection, to feel and express our fears, and to explore the possibility of ourselves as *interconnected*, as being a part of, not apart from, all of life. Inter-connectedness is a foundational belief that underpins the cultural traditions and spiritual practices of First Nations peoples across the globe and is central to contemporary eco-spiritual traditions.

On *Feeling-it Friday*, begin with simple rituals that encourage the knowing of feelings and the naming of fears. Have very young children share a rose (something positive), a thorn (something painful) and a banana peel (something funny). Go deeper with something silent and private; a ritual space to be alone together in the tenderness of unspoken emotion.

Make your home a place where feelings are freely shared. Maybe yours already is. But for many of us, being emotionally self expressed with our families can be challenging. Difficult emotions like despondency and despair can be so painful to witness that we are sometimes too quick to distract or lighten the mood. Emotions at the ugly end of the spectrum such as jealousy and anger are frequently discouraged, especially if they are being expressed loudly or in public or at an inappropriate time.

Use embodied rituals like dancing to encourage the full throttled feeling and expression of your collective feelings as a household. It might be how you are now or how you've felt through the week or your larger fears and feelings about the world. Compile a playlist by choosing a song each to capture your feelings. Play it loud. Feel the music and let it move you. Understand each other's emotions by feeling them in your bodies. Dance outside. Feel the earth. Feel fully. Grieve deeply. Express your anger, fear, despair, and feel them shift. Harness their power to fuel new action.

Day 6
Use your voice
Spread-the-word Saturday

Given the scale of our climate crisis, individual lifestyle changes alone will not save us. As citizens, we must also exert pressure on our governments to legislate for structural change. If history is anything to go by, then non-violent direct action is our best shot at forcing legislation for radical policy change on climate. According to research by Erica Chenoweth (cited in Robson, 2019), when sustained participation in nonviolent civil disobedience peaks at 3.5 percent of a population, it always succeeds in its cause. Where I live, in Melbourne, that's just 150,000 people, which means filling the Melbourne Cricket Ground just one and a half times. That seems manageable, doesn't it?

Or does it? Either way, from a climate consciousness perspective, the decision to use your voice has nothing to do with the odds of success.

Choosing to 'use your voice' is an *attitude*, one that grows courageously out of 'wanting to know.' To use your voice is to acknowledge that you have one, to feel whatever agency you have (however little it may be) and, with that, your responsibility to use it in the name of all who have none.

There are many ways to use your voice. Nonviolent direct action for policy change is certainly powerful, but remember, within the celebrated history of civil disobedience movements there are also important lessons about the limitations of the law to affect meaningful or lasting social change. In other words, radical policy change might bring us back from the brink of extinction but to secure our long term survival, we will need to change hearts and minds as well.

Whether through organised activism or your personal interactions, *Spread-the-word Saturday* invites you to use your voice with enthusiasm, buoyed by connection and community. Think of every enthusiastic sharing of your family's ongoing transformation as a form of direct action. On Saturdays, bring friends and other families together as a *7 Ways* community and use the voice of your experience to shepherd them safely to the learning edge of discomfort.

Encourage children to devote some of their weekends to youth climate activism or maybe find ways to engage as a family. You could kick off a climate art project, a campaign to declare a climate emergency, or an anti-consumerism clothes swap. Think expansively about the range of inequalities and injustices to which you might give voice to support the transition to climate consciousness. Find a way that speaks to each of you and lend your voices to the mass movement for change.

Day 7
Reflect
Slow Sunday

For many families, the multi-tasking-outcomes-focused rush of the day-to-day prevents deep connection. As a society, it prevents us from even noticing what is going on around us. We are far too busy. We simply don't have time to care about the experiences of our fellow humans, other species, or the planet.

Reflection is the process through which we *should* be able to learn from experience but the breakneck pace at which we live means there often isn't time. In its absence, we move blindly from one experience to the next, with the capacity to be neither discerning nor critical. If we do not reflect, we cannot effectively plan so we often find ourselves at the whim of other people's schedules. Our relationships can lack depth and stagnate because we do not make sense of interactions in between times.

When we reflect, we look back on our experiences to make sense of our actions. Reflection allows us to feel into feelings and uncover underlying attitudes that we may not have been aware of at the time. Unless we reflect, we do not entirely make sense to ourselves and nor does the world around us. We can remain stuck in unhelpful patterns of behaviour that we do not quite understand.

In many families, the rush of work life is replicated at home, with parents ferrying kids from one activity to the next in between helping with homework and household chores. Even when dinner is eaten as a family, the distraction of screens often means there's little conversation.

On *Slow Sunday*, we begin by slowing down, rejecting the consumerist obsession with speed. This alone makes slowness a symbolic act of resistance. More importantly, slowing down supports the awakening of our awareness. It gives us time to notice, to make sense of what we see, to care about it, and to remember to remain awake. In other words, it makes space for reflection.

Slow Sunday is a time to stop and take stock, to reflect on the *7 Ways* week just passed and your transition to climate consciousness. What have you learned? What have you felt? What have you done? What have you changed?

What more are you ready for? Try exploring these questions through embodied practices such as gardening, painting and dance. These are especially good for getting out of our heads and connecting with the attitudes and emotions underlying our thoughts and actions.

Record your reflections in a journal — or a blog, a photo-essay, or video — and encourage your kids to do the same. Share your reflections as a family and hatch some plans for the week ahead. But remember, reflection is not the same as problem solving or planning. Beware turning this into one more task on your to-do list. And don't forget to go slow.

Some final thoughts

The more young people I engage with about climate crisis, the more impressed I am. They are independent and resourceful thinkers and tenacious, determined activists. But what strikes me most when I see youth climate groups in action is their collaborative style of leadership and their gentle, inclusive approach. For these kinds of kids, who are comfortably making their own way to climate consciousness, your *7 Ways in 7 Days* practice may be less about helping *them* through the transition and more about helping *you* to stay out of their way. It might even be about getting more comfortable about acknowledging the wisdom of your children and nurturing their leadership by inviting *them* to guide your family's *7 Ways* practice.

Wherever your family is at and however you engage, I hope you are somehow supported by *7 Ways in 7 Days*. If you would like to share it, I would love to hear your story. Get in touch via the website **https://climate7.com/** where you can also download free *7 Ways* posters and other resources.

I acknowledge Aboriginal and Torres Strait Islander Peoples as the First Nations of Australia. They have never ceded sovereignty, and remain strong in their enduring connection to land and culture. I acknowledge their Elders past, present and emerging and that there can never be climate justice without First Nations justice.

References

Carrington, D 2018, 'Avoiding meat and dairy is "single biggest way" to reduce your impact on Earth,' *The Guardian*, 31 May, <https://www.theguardian.com/environment/2018/may/31/avoiding-meat-and-dairy-is-single-biggest-way-to-reduce-your-impact-on-earth>.

Clemons, R 2014, 'Fresh food tricks,' *Choice*, 15 September, <https://www.choice.com.au/shopping/everyday-shopping/supermarkets/articles/fresh-food-tricks>.

deeplygoodmag 2019, 'Food in the Anthropocene: new 'plant focused' diet could save the planet,' *deeplygoodmag*, <https://deeplygood.com/2019/02/20/food-in-the-anthropocene-new-plant-focused-diet-could-save-the-planet/?>.

Fawbert, D 2019 '"Eco-anxiety": how to spot it and what to do about it,' *BBC News*, 28 March, <https://www.bbc.co.uk/bbcthree/article/b2e7ee32-ad28-4ec4-89aa-a8b8c98f95a5>.

Haworth, A 2013, 'Why have young people in Japan stopped having sex?,' *The Guardian*, 20 October, <https://www.theguardian.com/world/2013/oct/20/young-people-japan-stopped-having-sex>.

McGowan, M 2018, 'Australian students feel lonelier and more left out than a decade ago,' *The Guardian*, 6 June, <https://www.theguardian.com/australia-news/2018/jun/07/australian-students-feel-lonelier-and-more-left-out-than-a-decade-ago>.

Monbiot, G 2014, 'The age of loneliness is killing us,' *The Guardian*, 14 October, <https://www.theguardian.com/commentisfree/2014/oct/14/age-of-loneliness-killing-us >.

Pariona, A 2017, 'The environmental impact of pesticides,' *worldatlas*, <https://www.worldatlas.com/articles/what-is-the-environmental-impact-of-pesticides.html>.

Robson, D 2019, 'The 3.5% rule: How a small minority can change the world,' *BBC Future*, 14 May, <http://www.bbc.com/future/story/20190513-it-only-takes-35-of-people-to-change-the-world>.

Sonesson, U, Davis, J, and Ziegler, F 2009, *Food production and emissions of greenhouse gases*, Food Climate Research Network, <https://www.fcrn.org.uk/sites/default/files/Food_production_and_GHGs.pdf>.

Weston, P 2019, 'The rise of eco-anxiety and how to come to terms with climate change,' *The Independent*, 22 June, <https://www.independent.co.uk/environment/climate-change-extinction-eco-anxiety-ice-melting-sea-level-wildfire-a8968011.html>.

Connecting with nature

Melinda Bito

> *"Teaching children about the natural world should be seen as one of the most important events in their lives."*
> Thomas Berry (1996)

SPENDING TIME in nature is not only beneficial for our children's health and wellbeing, it is essential for the healthy development of their body and mind.

Nature provides children with all the tools for learning, play, creativity and curiosity. With its ever-changing seasons and environment, nothing is ever the same, so children are constantly learning and discovering new things about it. When it rains, a child might discover a raindrop on a leaf or the depth of a puddle. During spring, they notice the flowers, the smells and the fruits growing on the trees. In summer, they feel the difference in the wind and sun. These experiences and feelings are what give them the deep connection to nature that takes them right through to adulthood.

If we don't connect with nature then we'll stop caring about nature, and what kind of future would that be? You only have to catch a train into the city to realise that people are so busy on their devices to even notice that spring has sprung or that the wattle has started to appear. The blossoms flower on the fruit trees and where there was once brown earth now lies a carpet of green. Are we at risk of losing a deep personal connection with the land and our own cultural practices? Are we losing our own seasonal rituals and ancient knowledge flows through our very veins?

There is an alarming and vast amount of scientific research on the benefits of nature for children, which indicates that exposure to nature has numerous long-term benefits both physically and mentally. Children that are presented with wide open spaces that are forever changing, which physically allows them to run, jump, and roll climb — exerting far more energy than being indoors — learn to take calculated risks which builds both self-confidence and resilience. Too many children these days are being diagnosed with ADHD or other sensory disorders but I wonder if they were given the time and space to just be outdoors, climbing, jumping, swinging and moving, would they still be so fidgety and restless indoors?

Children these days are spending most of their free time in structured and planned activities where they don't get to be spontaneous or creative — or just being present and at one with nature, something that many adults are trying to desperately to re-learn. This includes having exposure to sunlight and vitamin D which, in turn, has many positive effects including building a strong immune system. The great outdoors provides a sensory rich environment in which gross and fine motor skills are developed, along with sensory awareness. There is an alarming trend for children to stay indoors or not get dirty which has huge implications not only for their development but also their health given that dirt is said to have beneficial microbes that help build our child's immune system.

Emotional intelligence is another word that gets bounced around — the ability to manage the emotions of self and others, which adds to a child's overall wellbeing. In nature we are not confined to the same set of rules as we are indoors, whether it be at home or school. Outside, children can be freer to shout, run, squeal and laugh. They do not have to sit still or be confined by boundaries. This freedom to move and to express themselves can have tremendous benefits to ease anxieties and other tensions children can have.

I have, on many occasions, whilst observing and facilitating child led play, seen an 'energetic' or 'spirited' child slow down and immersive themselves in a water droplet on a leaf, or follow with curiosity a trail of ants up a tree. Likewise, I have watched quieter children, without pressure of social conformity, find themselves freely expressing through imaginative play. When children are connected with nature, they are more connected with themselves. A respect for each other is fostered and space to be able to explore emotions is found.

Playing in nature also brings forth the opportunity to examine life and death. The discovery of a dead bird or animal can bring inquisitive questions and the opportunity for discussion that may not be found in a classroom setting. Children learn empathy and fragility in a way which is very real and wondrous.

Intellectually, nature provides a treasure trove of resources and opportunity. Those of us wanting to make sure our STEM (science, technology, engineering, and maths) skill boxes are ticked don't have to go much further than local parks and reserves to find the many natural resources to help us do just that.

Sitting on the bank of a river we can watch which way the river flows, finding cut-down trees provides math opportunities, discovering how old the tree is by counting the rings, for example. Building a cubby or a bush swing covers the engineering aspect. Encouraging your child to keep a nature journal, looking up and noticing the clouds in the sky and many other similar activities. These simple activities not only will cover the first three aspects of STEM but will cultivate their connection to nature, and to be honest, it is also a lot of fun.

With every nature outing and each adventure we have with our children, we not only strengthen our bond with each but we strengthen our bond with this land and our cultural knowledge. We can educate and improve not only our children's but our own knowledge of the native flora and fauna and its uses. Foraging for bush foods is great place to start and gives a child purpose and may also build on their instinctive survival skills. It is always important to acknowledge the traditional custodians of the land you are on and understand their practices. Embedding traditional values and telling Dreamtime stories from your area will help us all to better appreciate the land we live on.

There is another more global reason as to why 'nature play' is so important to our children. Children hold the key to a sustainable future. One day they will grow up to become leaders and decision makers of their own. Connecting them to nature at an early stage of their lives is the key that could change our future.

As a parent and educator, I am aware of the enormity of the task ahead when it comes to climate change and the difficulties faced when trying to navigate the best way to explaining this to children without installing fear or worry. I asked this very question to director and film maker Damon Gameau who produced the documentary *2040* (Gameau, 2019). His answer was not to disguise or shy away from what has happened to our planet but to remain focused on what positive changes we can make and keep connected to nature. The fact is, for our children to start to gain an understanding about our planet and to start being inquisitive, we must simply allow them to connect with our environment by getting outdoors and playing.

The things that we care about are the exact things that we give our time and attention too. If we want our children to care about our environment and grow into adults who contribute to the solutions of our planet, we must give them ample time surrounded by nature and allow the wonders of learning in the natural world to flourish. During their formative years, children must be encouraged to develop respectful values of the natural wonders around them. For example, when a child understands the delicate design of a spiderweb they might be more careful of their surroundings; when they know the fragility of a tiny plant or insect, they will watch where they tread.

When our children are learning empathy through discovery, they are learning to care for the world around them. They are learning to care for the planet and the people on it.

From an early age children soon start to observe what should *not* be part of our natural world. Young children in particular will often pick up rubbish on walks or in parks. It is at this stage we have an opportunity to discuss why this should not be here and where should we put the rubbish. We can teach them to be part of the solution and not the problem, it can be so easy to just walk over the rubbish or ignore it. I know, I've been there, rushing to school drop-off. My daughter wanting to pick up a plastic bottle top. Part of me wanting to ignore it because we don't have time. We do have time, I made the time, because my child needs to know it is important, that this is the start of caring for our planet. Our children will learn from us, as we learned from our elders, so we will all learn from each other.

It may be hard to imagine what the next 20 years will look like especially for our children. I grew up in an era when there were no mobile phones, we knew it was time to go home for dinner when the sun started to go down and the streetlight came on. We ran free, we knew our neighbours and the news of an endangered species scared me. In the last 20 years technology advancements have changed our life and social media is anything but actually social.

With screen time a constant concern there also seems to be a desensitising of important matters. It is so easy these days to just scroll past the picture of a 'plastic island' in the ocean. It is fair to ask if people are really losing their grasp on what is real — or have they stop caring?

With an increase in technology, the decline in outdoor spaces (especially in suburban areas) and the fear of children taking risks, I believe it is imperative that we must start *now* to connect our children and ourselves back to nature.

Let's remind ourselves for our children's sake that we should really start to notice things again, to slow down and again notice things like the change in seasons, from winter to spring, summer then autumn. Not only do these moments provide great opportunities for discussion but there is also a deeper and more soulful effect as we start to understand the amazing natural rhythm of life. We can be relate this back to ourselves, our natural emotional state and energy cycle, our individual ebbs and flows. For example, the way in which we might feel energised in spring compared to winter when we are working internally on ourselves.

I strongly believe there is shift back to a simpler way of life that is less complicated and more in tune with nature. I watch as families spend more time together outdoors, I observe how much more relaxed we all are.

This is no coincidence, you see, in our connection to each other. Our families and our land are put into perspective when we are in the great outdoors. We are forced into the present moment, into the here and now. There is no pile of laundry, no dirty dishes, no laptop pinging with notifications from work. We are just here in the present moment and, as if by magic, everything suddenly seems a bit easier. Society's unrealistic expectations are lifted. Our connection and attention to each other is stronger because, for that moment, you are not distracted. The fresh air literally cleanses you and the sunshine eases your tensions. If you have ever been to the ocean and breathed in the salty fresh air or stood with your bare feet on the soft moss of the forest floor, then you will know what I'm talking about.

Nature is medicine, it is beneficial if not crucial to our mental health and wellbeing and I can't think of a better place to raise our future generations.

Note

Resources to encourage outside play and discovery of nature can be found at: https://www.natureplay.org.au/

References

Berry, T 1996, *Creative Energy: Bearing Witness for the Earth*, Sierra Club Books, San Francisco.

Gameau, D 2019, *2040* [documentary film], <https://www.madmanfilms.com.au/.

Connection — the power of 'us'

Robin Grille

IT WASN'T LIKE this when I was a schoolboy. Our emotional wellbeing barely rated a mention — at least that's how it seemed to me. There was no talk of child-centred education or the importance of EQ (Emotional Quotient). Today, emotional wellness is the talk of the town, sometimes rhetorically, sometimes genuinely. Educationists scramble to teach our youth how they can bolster their bounce-back and restock their emotional strengths. 'Resilience' — the buzz word of the age and *dernier cri* in educational settings — is a word that ranks highly in child-rearing colloquy and departmental declarations.

But are we all on the same page about where resilience comes from? What unspoken assumptions animate our newfound preoccupation with this faculty? Are children born with a deficit of resilience, depending on us, their elders, to teach them its secrets? Is resilience a thing to be taught? Or perhaps is it a natural faculty, eroded by the way children are enculturated?

Judging by how widely the talk of 'resilience' has permeated the chat-o-sphere, there must be a collective worry that it is in short supply. We certainly seem afraid that there is not enough of it about. Is psychological frailty natural, or is it a symptom of a failing society? Well might we be known for our good cheer and sunny dispositions, but Australians have the second highest prevalence of depressive disorders in the world, a position we share with the USA, the wealthiest and most powerful country on earth (World Health Organization, 2017). Over one in 20 people are depressed, and the rate is rising. Worldwide, depression is now the leading cause of ill health and disability. And if we are not depressed, we are afraid. One in seven of us are embattled with anxiety disorders.

Every day in Australia, eight people take their own lives. In one year over 65,000 Australians attempt suicide. We are at a 10-year peak and the rate is rising for young and old, even for children under 14-years-old. We like to think we have it all, but the stark truth is that unbearable misery abounds. Modern lifestyle is now our biggest killer. Lifestyle diseases such as diabetes, obesity, heart disease and some cancers are at epidemic levels globally, they top the charts as leading causes of death and the rates are increasing dramatically.

So, we create programs to teach resilience and emotional intelligence to our children. Without a doubt, this is a huge leap forward from the detachment and emotional illiteracy that prevailed in my school years. But what if the cause of our brokenness is systemic? Will our wellness courses for individuals make the difference for the broader population?

In a time of climate emergency, just when our children's resilience will be most severely tested, an epidemic of melancholy is sweeping the globe. Simultaneously, we seem struck with a blindness that lets us accelerate unswervingly towards a precipice of ecocide. Twin symptoms of modernity: a spiralling emotional malaise and a madness that permits business-as-usual in times of environmental catastrophe. Could both be caused by the same thing?

How did we come to be so morose, so alienated from one another? How did we manage to create an eco-apocalyptic scenario — and are these two nightmares linked? Could it be that the same thing that undermines children's emotional health has also made us an ecocidal species? Conversely, could the medicine that restores our youth's emotional health simultaneously be what creates the eco-harmonious society?

The roots of detachment

Until recently we the 'modern' have revelled in hubris; a collective self-assurance bordering on gloating about how well we seemed to be doing. Full of techno-confidence, we were riding high. Industrial and social progress promised to free us from disease, discomfort, toil, inconvenience, insecurity and the elements. We walked on the moon! Nothing could halt our steady march towards conquering Nature itself.

How wide-eyed and innocent our love-affair with fast cars and gleaming gadgetry seems now, in the age of fracking and plastic islands. We are not feeling quite so cocky about human 'progress,' as a pervasive sense that something is terribly wrong sweeps the globe. There is a growing disquiet, a gnawing realisation that we've poisoned our well. Trust in civil institutions is at an all-time low; only one in five people believe 'the system' is working for them. Trust in media, government and banks is in terminal decline (Edelman, 2019).

For sure, we can fly and enjoy comforts, convenience and abundance the likes of which our forebears could not have imagined. But to have this we've unleashed mass extinction, an insect apocalypse, plastic rain and climate chaos. As the oceans rise, our evermore frantic climate scientists place our destiny on a slippery cliff-edge. Their sombre prognosis: 10 years to the point of no return.

Today we face the first existential threat to every human on earth since the Cuban Missile Crisis of 1962 — but the current ecological crisis cannot be so quickly defused. How wounded must we be, how bereft and disconnected to have become so careless and self-defeating? Still our emissions rise each year. It has to be said: this is a form of insanity. A deep crack in our collective emotional intelligence now seems likely to extinguish civilisation as we know it.

None of this doomsday scenario was inevitable. For some time now the most toxic production and energy generation systems have been largely optional. Countless opportunities to transition to renewable and sustainable practice were squandered. Our impediment is not technological; it is *psychological*.

What has caused us to be so detached? What is the nature of this collective wound, and how can we help our young to be emotionally healthier than their predecessors? For certain, our children will need all the resilience they can muster to pull through in the unravelling of our civilisation's operating system. So, are we meant to *teach* resilience to our children, or would they be better served if we reform the child-rearing customs that rob their resilience in the first place? And what if the same child-rearing reforms that restore emotional health are precisely what is needed to heal our ecocidal illness? Can we boost resilience and save the planet with the same stroke?

I believe the same culprit that plunged us into planetary emergency is also behind the erosion of emotional intelligence. We share a deep and common emotional wound: the legacy of millennia of customary child abuse and neglect that spanned the continents. The history of childhood has been, until recently, an unacknowledged litany of horrors.

I chronicled the surprising ubiquity of violence and neglect towards children in *Parenting for a Peaceful World* (Grille, 2013). A glimpse at what most people suffered in their early years is as shocking as it is enlightening. Through a neuroscientific, trauma-informed, lens, this sobering but inescapable realisation comes into focus: humanity itself is an abuse survivor, and is currently in recovery. Humanity as a whole suffers from Post-Traumatic Stress Disorder (PTSD), but most of us don't know it. The bulk of this relational trauma is from childhood, transmitted intergenerationally. Having been normalised and camouflaged as 'culture,' collective trauma is barely recognised or validated.

To know how to lift our children from the current quagmire, it helps first to understand the historic depredation of our own and our forebears' emotional health. Our fundamental wound involves the loss of connection; to our deepest selves, to one another, to the biosphere and our non-human family. Humanity feels acutely alone, abandoned, threatened and suspicious. We have come to accept this existential emptiness as *normal*; the default flavour of existence. The societies we create are the symptoms of this collective PTSD.

When desperate greed and pillage rules the world, it's a mistake to say: "…therefore humans are largely selfish and violent." This does not define humanity, it defines *wounded* humanity — humanity driven mad through generations of traumatic disconnection. We have yet to see the kind of civilisation that would spring from a predominant child-rearing mode that truly meets children's emotional needs.

The same process that would restore our children's emotional health and psychological resilience is the one that will transform us into an ecologically harmonious species. Connection is the central theme. But before we investigate what would help our children be more resilient, we should look at how to stop subverting the development of natural, emotional wellness. Do we teach our children resilience from a text? Or revise the child-rearing and educational systems that undermined it? Zooming-in for a close look at how we got into the current mess may give us the best clues about the necessary paradigm shift.

The culture of separateness

What kind of world can our children expect to find when they finally leave their studies — and how has education contrived to make our children conform with this world?

In the Age of Individualism, the primacy of the individual has reached its apotheosis. Psychology's chief objectives are *self*-improvement and *self*-actualisation, and developmental theories are almost entirely about the psychology of the individual. Seldom has psychology concerned itself with relationships and the ecology of community.

Not that we would want to go back to old times. The constitutional protections of individual expression were a welcome leap forward in social evolution. No one in their right mind would want a return to the days of the divine right of kings and the theocratic barbarism in which a divergent opinion would earn you hours of torment on a pyre.

But somewhere along the line we lost our balance. The Age of Individualism has borne fruit and its fruit is rotting. Today there is no self-indulgence, no abrogation of social consciousness and no petty tribalism that stand as a bar to national leadership. It would seem narcissism is more than enough of a qualification.

The hard-won 'freedom' of the modern era has been co-opted to mean 'anything goes, in the pursuit of profit.' Like a mob at a department store sale, we've trampled connectedness, social-responsibility and altruism underfoot. Almost by stealth, free-market fanaticism metastasised from a marginal, post-second world war economic doctrine into today's unchallenged cultural assumption (Stedman Jones, 2014).

We are living at the zenith of a worldwide economic orthodoxy that elevates self-service above all else. From the classical economist, Adam Smith (1776), to recent Nobel laureates like James M Buchanan and Milton Friedman, the gurus of self-centred economics have persuaded policy makers everywhere that human beings are almost exclusively driven by self-interest. This is hardly an idle claim; since neoliberalism has become the dominant school of thought in global and national institutions. Thinkers such as Buchanan and Friedman were the godfathers of the 'greed is good' way of doing business. To the Bishops of the Church of the Free-Market, we are a 'me-first' species and, if they have their way in business and education policy, so we must remain.

Not only has neoliberalism made a religion of narcissism, it is openly and morbidly suspicious of sharing and community, which are ad nauseam compared to Stalinism or Nazism. Feathering one's nest and defeating our rivals is, supposedly, what makes us all tick. Put greed to work, they say, and the economy will steam along like a happy Puffing Billy train. This business model has become a way of life, the new world order. It is chilling to consider how quickly such a bleak and unsubstantiated version of psychology can become canon, if repeated often enough.

With the influence of corporate-funded think tanks, the neoliberal philosophy became immensely influential until the creed of privatising as many public services and assets as possible and deregulating everything enveloped the western world. All is for profit, no rules apply. The markets, not those we elect, must decide our fate. And since greed is now the uncontested driver of economies, trade and politics; connectedness and ecology are relegated to weekend luxuries at best.

Self-interest is the 'x' in all economic formulas. The gears of society now turn on the fumes of narcissism. What does this mean for human relations? For a start, when the global economy and its institutions have bet on selfishness as its currency, it pits us against one another. Parents everywhere anticipate an increasingly harsh and competitive world and accordingly they fret over how to inure their children for it. They certainly don't anticipate a world based on collaboration to greet their children as they leave school. An almost survivalist view of 'success' eclipses passion-led education. This injects an unnecessary, health-sapping frenzy into a life-stage that should be joyous — the antithesis, surely, of what is needed for emotional wellness. What is this doing to our children?

Far from being scientific, neoliberal theories of human motivation are delinquent of conventional neurobiology. The brain's empathy circuits and mirror neurones are Nature's design to make us exquisitely attuned to the feelings of others (Cozolino, 2017; Baron-Cohen, 2011; Szalavitz and Perry, 2010).

Our biology craves interpersonal connection, we are wired for altruism. In healthy individuals, generosity lights up the brain's reward centres. But the synaptic webs that animate empathy are left to atrophy in a culture that favours separateness. Since connectedness is the heart of emotional wellness, this new global order mitigates against resilience. First, we fashion a culture that pressures children to abandon their hearts in the tactical pursuit of accumulation, advantage and image. Then, we try to brace our youth's resilience against a socio-economic current that dismantles the very communitas on which it depends.

When markets gobble up the commons, nothing is sacred. We've even outsourced parenting, leaving our babies in the 'care' of for-profit corporates. At the critical stage when meeting a child's attachment needs is developmentally most vital, all that is foundational for emotional resilience goes out the window (Biddulph, 2006). Secure familial attachments, according to the scientific consensus, are the very heartbeat of human resilience. When children endure separation from their loved ones too early, too often and for too long, this stokes the risk of illness, depression, addiction or violence for the long term (Fonagy, Target, Steele & Steele, 1997; Belsky & Cassidy, 1994; Gerhardt, 2004).

The largest epidemiological study of the long-term impact of early childhood experience (Felitti *et al*,1998) has emphatically confirmed the nurture of children as *the* most powerful factor in psychological health, and a range of physiological outcomes involving cardiac, respiratory, oncological and digestive health. It's not what we *teach* children, but how we *treat* them, that makes the real difference in the long term.

Today's economic order is the antithesis of what brings us our emotional health. Along with our alienation from our essential biology, we have also lost our sense of ecological belongingness. We the 'civilised' don't see ourselves as part of the earth, we are its *masters*. No conventional economic equation includes the biosphere as a variable. We do business in the delusion of a limitless environment, eternally available for our plunder and waste. The technologies necessary for a circular economy (zero-waste, fully recyclable or degradable production, and regenerative agriculture) are already with us (Wikipedia, 2019[1]). But we drag our feet, clinging obstinately to our fancied position of dominion over everything. This is imperilling our viability on this earth.

We may not care to admit it, but grandiosity sits alongside narcissism as structural pillars of our style of civilisation. How has this psychopathic society — and the expectations that come with it — affected our children's development? Let's take a look.

The role of education

How have society's patriarchs convinced entire populations to fall in line with our self-serving and eco-unfriendly ways? By daily training our children to think, live and react accordingly. Education is not a given; it has always been tailored to serve the prevailing requirements of industry and the economic rationales of the day. In other words, the economic philosophies of the era can be seen reflected in the predominant style of schooling. A self-interest economy ensures mass compliance via education styles calculated to prepare children to compete against rivals and to exploit natural systems rather than belong within them. True commitments to a circular economy and enjoyable work have not yet made much of an inroad into mainstream curricula. Learning is by compulsion, at the behest of an unquestionable authority.

Teachers both choose and direct courses for all until late in high school — and even then the student has minimal input into daily rhythms or curriculum content. Students are, by hook or by crook, moulded into a national standard. In a culture of examination and rankings, motivation is too often secured through fear and shame (Kohn, [n.d.]). Children are directed to perceive through the frame of 'success,' rather than trusting what they love to do. This top-down organisational culture in school creates its own reflection in the broader society.

Resilience cannot properly thrive in an educational environment that shows little curiosity about each child's unique gifts and passions, and instead conditions them to endure drudgery. We become resilient when connected to our passion and purpose. I doubt we can transition to a new kind of ecologically harmonious and peaceful society simply by tweaking technology or the stock market. Transition has its roots in the way we listen to our children's deepest feelings, so it must begin with passion-based education; an education based on love.

As yet there are few education systems that truly ask each child what they love; what their natural interests are. We tell them what to know, we don't ask them who they are. We shape their aspirations for them. We tell them where to go and when, we tell them what to learn and how. And then we lament their lack of self-motivation. When we teach children that work is the opposite of play, when we lure them towards the pursuit of money rather than nurture their love of work, we disconnect them from their own hearts. This traditional approach robs resilience of its oxygen, it is a recipe for depression and alienation.

Individuals who have not been helped to pursue their true vocation tend to accept careers for which they have no love. Around the word, little over one in ten people polled say they like going to work (McGregor, 2013). Most people have absorbed the message that work is a kind of necessary suffering to be avoided if possible. Monday is for Monday-itis, and on Fridays we thank God. This is a colossal, demographic tragedy, and it exacts an enormous toll on mental health and the planet.

Desperately dreaming of an early escape from drudgery we speculate and gamble. Stock and currency markets operate like a casino, where the desperate bet their lives on a wheel of boom-and-bust. In vain attempts to fill our cavernous inner emptiness, we consume, hoard and waste. A population of work-averse individuals places impossible pressures on the biosphere. This is hardly a recipe for an Earth-respecting culture. It is even less a recipe for joy or emotional wellness. Our work is killing us — and our schools are complicit.

If we are not supported to locate and follow our true vocational passions we lose an inner sanctum that can preserve our sanity and vitality, renew our spirit and make us indomitable in the face of failure, loss or tragedy. We are far more resilient when we are well-connected to ourselves; when we know what we love and we do it for a living. For those lucky enough to love their work, life is rich with meaning and work feels like a mission.

A transitional society based on ecologically-sound social and economic principles is unlikely unless we reinvent education and rethink its objectives. Standardisation, coercion, ranking and the presumption of competition fail to connect with children's hearts. Lip-service to 'child-centredness' and spin about 'emotional intelligence' have gained traction but will remain fads until children are supported and encouraged to learn playfully and passionately.

If we are to prepare our children for a new kind of future-proof, transitional society, we need to help them know themselves, to study according to their natural passions, to be collaborators and to be fully conscious of their valued place in an interdependent world.

Education for transition

The vintage system of homework, enforcement, exams, and universal standards is defunct — and it's time to ditch it. A new educational imperative is gaining ground around the world, based on diverse experimental approaches to an *emergent curriculum*. As the name suggests, the learning adventure emerges uniquely from inside each child. In this model the teacher acts as midwife, mentor and consultant — rather than director and judge. Power is decentralised, standards are unlocked and this dispenses creative freedom to each teacher-student dyad. A mind-boggling proposal perhaps, to a traditionalist — but in a historic moment when business-as-usual is endangering our survival, a little boggling of minds might be called for. Is the emergent curriculum a fit of fanciful idealism, or a stroke of practical realism?

Finland, a country known for leading the world in academic achievement, famously uses an emergent curriculum approach. If you can imagine children being helped to choose what to learn, how to learn it and where to learn it, then you are imagining the *democratic* schools (from pre-school to high-school) that have been flourishing in Israel, across Europe, Asia, New Zealand and Australia, the Free School system in Japan, the Sudbury system in USA, even the Catholic primary schools of inner Sydney. The list has grown too long to summarise.

Since 1993, the International Democratic Education Conference has taken place each year in a different country. It is a broad and inclusive church with a vibrant array of approaches and a sliding scale of relative freedoms for students. An international movement abuzz with multi-cultural enthusiasm, *democratic education* has amassed an impressive track-record of academic accomplishment, as well as transformative impacts on surrounding communities. Across the world people grow daily more disillusioned with the old system, so the ranks of progressive education are bursting. With growing support from municipal and national governments, child-led education is becoming commonplace. Judging by the flow of positive data and academic endorsements, its drift into the mainstream seems all but inevitable (Grille, 2011).

Many are surprised by what they see in a democratic classroom, when they visit for the first time. When learning ceases to be mandatory, far from this resulting in a festival of foot-dragging and chaos, children generally tackle their studies with avid intensity. There is a particular emphasis on inquiry-based projects that require collaborative group-work. Uninterrupted by the blast of a horn or the clanging of bells every 40 minutes, students have the space to become immersed in their subject for as long as they need. These are the conditions that enable that precious state of *flow*; in which the student becomes deeply absorbed, at one with their activity, in a state of complete focus. Psychologists have discovered that these trance-like *flow-states* maximise productivity. Flow-states enhance memory retention, creativity and problem-solving abilities.

But flow-states, if experienced regularly enough, offer far more than cognitive advantages. They are essential for emotional wellbeing, they constitute a key ingredient for resilience (Csikszentmihalyi, 2008). Flow-states are no luxury. Without knowing how to access these serene and hyper-productive states, it is as if we are living with a handbrake on. In a state of flow, study and work can feel profoundly fulfilling, at times exhilarating. When we are routinely shunted from classroom to classroom and made to read, memorise or listen to what we have no interest in, entering flow is nigh impossible. The freedom to choose subjects we love is an essential condition. The emergent curriculum is fundamental to a healthy society.

Perhaps the most exciting outcome of democratic education is one that was entirely unexpected. It has been a common finding for democratic educators the world over that the incidence of bullying and school violence has tumbled in their schools. So reliable is this result, that democratic education has begun to be used strategically as a treatment for social violence. Though it took two years to do it, the most violent school in Tel Aviv was transformed into the happiest by an incoming team of democratic educators (Hecht, 2012). Unsurprisingly Finland, with its nationwide democratic education culture, enjoys low rates of violent crime, has been listed as the happiest country (Wikipedia 2019[2]), and has the lowest rate of political corruption on the world. The regular availability of flow-states yields a peace dividend, with obvious implications for a transitional society.

I believe that if a young person emerges from school having no idea what they want to do for a living, having no love for work and having no passion for further learning, then the school system has failed them. If children emerge from school not knowing how to achieve flow-states, the school has left them psychologically vulnerable.

Conversely, children whose true vocation and gifts have been supported are far more likely to love contributing, to have a deep social and environmental conscience and to take pleasure from their work. They are less likely to be violent, depressed, addicted or materialistic. Many more would want to remain productive past their 'retirement age,' sharply reducing the doom-and-gloom predictions about an ageing (and presumably helpless) population.

The right to choose a beloved vocation is the bottom-line of a new society based on non-violent institutions, a circular economy, and a felt sense of belonging to the human family. Our children deserve better than to resiliently endure the collapse of ecosystems and markets. Connected young people can be the co-creators of a new, paradigm-shifting society that takes humanity into a viable, beautiful and ecologically harmonious future. A society where freedom of expression does not mean a license to profit and hoard without limit. A society where individual freedom is balanced with responsibility, connectedness and love.

The power of listening

Emotional wellness is proportional to our sense of connection — to ourselves, to others and to the world around us. Feeling connected at school is an essential — but not sufficient — ingredient for our children's emotional health. Too intangible and subjective to define or measure, interpersonal connection depends on the authentic communication of emotion. Firstly and most importantly, this is about *listening*. Our children's emotional security is, at its most fundamental, about how well their feelings are heard, understood and validated.

When someone listens to our deepest feelings without judgment or advice, we immediately feel closer to them. We feel less alone in the world. Our bodies register this ineffable moment of bonding; there is a softening of the chest, a melting of the heart, a tingle in the solar plexus. Our breathing deepens, our exhalation lengthens. Our shoulders relax. In this moment of connection, we feel like we've come home.

When we listen openly to one another, especially when sharing emotion, a brain scan would show the empathy centres of our brains lighting up. Oxytocin, the hormone of love, is released into the bloodstream, infusing us with a general sense of wellbeing and uplift. Neuroscience has taken human empathy beyond the domain of poetry. Empathy is the real medicine. It is the cornerstone of our resilience and without enough of it, we break. If we want the next generation to be strong, self-secure and emotionally intelligent, our top priority is to hear their voices and respond empathically, from their very first day of life.

There is a great deficit of good listening in our world. It's not that listening is a complicated art, but rather, we are afraid to hear our children's feelings. We press them to be cheerful, to 'think positive,' We suppress their anger. We shame them for their fear, tell them to 'get over it,' and override their shyness. We ignore their neediness. How often we block their messages, making the empathic connection impossible.

But it's not as if our barriers are not understandable. Parents and teachers are too-often overwhelmed, under-supported and stressed. It is human to be limited. More to the point, it is our own feelings we are afraid of. As creatures wired for empathy, our children's pain can be unbearable to us to the point that we turn away, or do our best to talk them out of their experience. To run from our own helplessness, we shut our children's emotions down, or at least swerve around them.

As parents, teachers and elders we can all afford to brush-up on our listening skills. Very few of us have benefitted from good role models for listening. I believe we can change the world, one child at a time, by learning to be better listeners than our antecedents. There is every reason to trust the healing power of listening, because an emotion that is validated is an emotion that is transformed.

Emotions do not stand still. When any of us feels seen and heard, this immediately settles our hearts. Exactly the same is true for children. Moreover, when children live in an environment in which they feel emotionally safe, they become more self-assured, more caring and more resilient. Conversely, when an emotion is blocked, it is put aside or repressed and thus it persists. Listening at first takes courage — at times, great courage — but when we dare to listen, it changes everything.

Listening well does not mean (by any stretch!) being permissive towards any behaviour. This distinction is critical: we can say 'yes' to emotion, while at the same time saying 'no' to behaviour. For example, we can stop siblings from fighting and emphatically demand a cease-fire — but that does not preclude us sitting with each combatant afterwards, and listening intently to what had made them angry. Validating our children's emotions is precisely what sets them on a developmental path away from violence. That is why good listening is the prime tool of conflict resolution, in parenting, education, in organisations and, in fact, in every setting.

As a foundational factor for wellbeing, the need for attuned listening starts from the dawn of a child's life. Today's scientific consensus is that secure attachment, defined by warm, consistent and warm responsiveness to babies' needs, is the mainstay of psychological and physiological health (Australian Association for Infant Mental Health Inc. 2016). From early childhood onwards, a secure emotional connection with carers offers children long-lasting protection from depression, anxiety, aggressiveness and a host of stress-related diseases such as cardiac, respiratory, inflammatory and digestive disorders and some cancers. Secure attachment in childhood is also the main determining factor behind the way we cope with stress, cushioning us for life against the worst effects of PTSD, even after serious trauma (Ogle, Rubin and Siegler, 2015). Secure early attachment is, by definition, the keystone of resilience.

The most compelling testament to the power of good listening comes from demonstrations in the field, where results can be dramatic. Australian psychologists Robyn Dolby and Belinda Swan trained the early childhood staff at one of inner-Sydney's most deeply troubled preschools to listen unconditionally to their children's wild array of emotions, to offer their steady presence and acceptance and refrain from compulsive advice or intervention. The reduction in behavioural incidents that resulted came so rapidly and so steeply, even the experimenters were surprised. Their greatest expectations were exceeded. Soon, even the high staff turnover rates settled down as carers enjoyed the restoration of order that their consistent and empathic availability had brought about.

Australian psychologist, Dr Vicky Flory, set out to investigate the healing power of attuned listening by testing it as a treatment for children suffering the most acute and chronic psychiatric disorders (Flory, 2005). Flory's researchers did not treat the ailing children but, instead, focused on their parents; training them to listen empathically, helping them be more aware of their child's distress, and challenging their negative judgments about their children's behaviour. The children's symptoms were significantly reduced (Flory, 2004). When children's feelings, aspirations and dreams are heard and validated, the course of their lives is altered.

Good listening, at home and at school, is the fountainhead of personal and social, paradigm-shifting transformation. Of course, good listening is not the only resilience-building strategy and there are plenty more, beyond the scope of this essay. But validation of a child's emotional world is basic to their feeling connected, and connection is the marrow of wellness.

Two problems, one solution

The mode of society that has sought dominion over the earth is not inevitable. It is optional. It is optional that we view those from different 'tribes' as rivals. It is optional to hitch our self-identity to nationalistic zealotry.

The 'take-make-waste' extractive industrial model is not the only way to feed, clothe and house ourselves. And it is audacious to believe we are the masters of Nature rather than its dependants.

If our modes of production are riddled with delusion this is because our society is built of disconnection, it is symptomatic of millennia of collective trauma. If we are to escape this obsolete manner of civilisation, education systems and child-rearing modes must be reformed. Resilience and emotional intelligence are not text-book subjects, they are relationship styles and must be modelled if they are to be fostered. Emotional intelligence is a bodily skill, not a philosophy.

A borderless, warless world relying on circular economies and regenerative agriculture — these are entirely achievable realities. The necessary technologies are already here, developing further every day, and re-tooling is now a survival imperative.

Let's allow ourselves to imagine a new future. What would our economies and our social institutions look like if they could spring from a base of interconnectedness and emotional intelligence? One thing for sure, this 'future-kind' of society would be radically — and beautifully — different to what we have today. Our individual uniqueness is to be nurtured, protected and celebrated. But it is only one pole of existence. Balance and health require an equal devotion to that part of ourselves that is 'us,' that part of ourselves that longs to contribute to community, to know we entwine with our non-human family, to revere our Natural home. The joy of full individual expression seeks balance with the bliss of interconnectedness.

The onus is on us, the elders, to feed our children's sense of connection; by truly listening to and validating their emotions, their dreams and aspirations. What strengthens our children's hearts is simultaneously what will create the *Future-kind* of society that must now be formed.

References

Australian Association for Infant Mental Health Inc. 2016, *Responding to Babies' Cues, Australian: Position Paper 2*, Australian Association for Infant Mental Health Inc., Double Bay, NSW. [<https://www.aaimhi.org/key-issues/position-statements-and-guidelines/AAIMHI-Position-paper-2-(2016)-Responding-to-infant-cues-(1).pdf>]

Baron-Cohen, S 2011, *The Science of Evil: On Empathy and the Origins of Cruelty*, Basic Books, New York.

Belsky, J & Cassidy, J 1994, 'Attachment: Theory and evidence,' in Rutter M & Hay D F (eds), *Development Through Life: A Handbook for Clinicians*, Blackwell Scientific, Boston, pp 373-401.

Biddulph, S 2006, *Raising Babies – Why your Love is Best*, Harper Thorsons, Sydney.

Csikszentmihalyi, M 2008, *Flow: the Psychology of Optimal Experience HarperCollins*, rev. edn., New York.

Cozolino, L 2017, *The Neuroscience of psychotherapy: Healing the social brain*, 3rd edn, WW Norton & Co, New York.

Dolby, R 2017, *The Circle of Security: Roadmap to building supportive relationships*, Early Childhood Australia, Fyshwick, Australia Capital Territory.

Edelman 2019, *2019 Edelman Trust Barometer: Global Report*, Edelman, New York, <https://www.edelman.com/trust-barometer>.

Felitti, V J *et al* 1998, 'Relationship of Childhood Abuse and Household Dysfunction to Many of the Leading Causes of Death in Adults,' *American Journal of Preventive Medicine*, vol. 14, no. 4, pp 245-258.

Flory, V 2004, 'A novel clinical intervention for severe childhood depression and anxiety,' *Clinical Child Psychology and Psychiatry*, vol. 9, no.1, pp. 9–23.

Flory, V 2005, *Your Child's Emotional Needs: What They Are and How to Meet Them*, Finch Publishing, Sydney.

Fonagy, P, Target, M, Steele, M & Steele, H 1997, 'The development of violence and crime as it relates to security of attachment' in Osofsky, J D (ed.) *Children in a Violent Society*, Guilford Press, New York, pp.150-177.

Gerhardt, S 2004, *Why Love Matters: How Affection Shapes a Baby's Brain*, Brunner-Routledge and Hove, New York.

Grille, R 2011, 'The School of World Peace,' in Wright D, Camden-Pratt C E & Hill S B (eds), *Social Ecology*, Hawthorne Press, Stroud, Gloucestershire, UK. [Chapter 17]

Grille, R 2013, *Parenting for a Peaceful World*, Vox Cordis Press, Sydney.

Hecht, Y 2012, *Democratic Education: a Beginning of a Story*, Alternative Education Resource Organization, Roslyn Heights, New York.

Kohn, A [n.d.], *'No Grades + No Homework = Better Learning,'* alfiekohn.org, <https://www.alfiekohn.org/grades-homework-better-learning/>.

McGregor, J 2013, 'Only 13 percent of people worldwide actually like going to work,' *Washington Post*, 10 October 2013, <https://www.washingtonpost.com/news/on-leadership/wp/2013/10/10/only-13-percent-of-people-worldwide-actually-like-going-to-work/?>.

Ogle, C M, Rubin, D C & Siegler, I C 2015, 'The Relation Between Insecure Attachment and Posttraumatic Stress: Early Life Versus Adulthood Traumas,' *Psychological Trauma: Research, Practice, and Policy*, vol. 7, no. 4, pp. 324–332.

Smith, A 1776, *The Wealth of Nations* [Books I-V], William Strachan, London.

Stedman Jones, D 2014, *Masters of the Universe: Hayek, Friedman, and the Birth of Neoliberal Politics*, Princeton University Press, Princeton, New Jersey.

Szalavitz, M & Perry, B D 2010, *Born for Love: Why Empathy is Essential — and Endangered*, HarperCollins, New York.

Wikipedia 2019 [1], 'Cradle-to-Cradle Design,' *Wikipedia*, <https://en.wikipedia.org/wiki/Cradle-to-cradle_design>.

Wikipedia 2019 [2], 'World Happiness Report,' *Wikipedia*, <https://en.wikipedia.org/wiki/World_Happiness_Report>.

Winston, R & Chicot, R 2016, 'The importance of early bonding on the long-term mental health and resilience of children,' *London Journal of Primary Care*, vol. 8, no.1, pp 12-14.

World Health Organization 2017, *Depression and Other Common Mental Disorders: Global Health Estimates*, World Health Organization, Geneva, Switzerland, <https://www.who.int/mental_health/management/depression/prevalence_global_health_estimates/en/>.

Trust: the currency of childhood

Brigitte Kupfer

THIS IS HOW John Holt, an educational reformer and social critic, described his book *How Children Learn*:

> All I am saying can be summed up in two words: TRUST CHILDREN. Nothing could be more simple, or more difficult. Difficult because to trust children we must first learn to trust ourselves, and most of us were taught as children that we could not be trusted. (Holt, 1983)

Trusting our children and trusting ourselves? Does this sound crazy when we consider what global threats we are facing and that humanity's survival is in question? What if the craziness lies in putting our trust in (technological) solutions which are supposed to 'save' us, but leave out the basic building blocks of all our lives: trusting caring relationships?

What if the future lies in the relationship between the generations? We are living on a troubled planet in troubled times. Our public institutions of Government, Health and Education are moving towards reliance on technology more than on building trusting relationships. But all over the world people find each other and get together to weave new structures in regenerative projects, midwifing a new story for humanity and hospicing the old.

We live "between stories" as Charles Eisenstein says (Eisenstein, 2013). Joanna Macy (2012 and 2014) and David Korten (2007) have talked about our time as "The Great Turning." Much is written about the paradigm change from a mechanistic linear machine-like worldview to an inter-connected living systems view of our world.

A transformation of the status quo cannot happen until we recognise that the story we have been living by has deeply misled us. It is a story of alienation from ourselves and each other and the living world around us. This blindness is the driver of the destructive path we are on. Our relationship with the world is a mirror of the relationship we have with ourselves, with our own bodies.

The connection with our children reflects the connection with our bodies, and the future depends on no longer agreeing to be shaped by societal structures which violate our bodies' intelligence. The future is not in the hand of the next generation. It is in the hands of the relationship between the generations. Parenting is where the future happens.

As Philip Shepherd says:

> What is being asked of us is not a little thing. It is not an add-on or an adjustment to our way of being; it is a different way of being; it is a revolution in consciousness. This journey into wholeness is a revolution that the entire planet is crying out for — and it can only begin with individuals like you making a personal choice. (Shepherd, 2019)

One of these personal choices was when I walked out of my obstetrician's office, knowing I wouldn't be back. I was in the second half of my pregnancy and I wanted to discuss the possibility of a home birth. Her prompt response was "Let's not go there. I am here to look after you."

It felt patronising and wrong. No, it was not rebellion and I was not playing hero. I had come to explore my options. I knew that it was I who was the most important person in the room concerned with the future of my child. I was the whole world for my baby at that time. My body was his home. What I thought, felt and acted on mattered to my baby literally. I was the one looking after me and my baby with the support of my partner and friends.

Nothing was wrong with me. I felt in right relationship with my baby and I had learned to trust myself. To paraphrase the philosopher Goethe from a few hundred years ago: *"As soon as you trust yourself, you will know how to live."* And I think we also can say: "As soon as you trust yourself, you know how to birth and you know how to parent."

This is however not the usual advice parents receive in our globalised capitalist economy. The products and services advertised and sold to us to overcome our 'deficiencies' by health and education industries with their unquestioned self-improvement ideology, are keeping our focus on 'what is wrong?' and 'what could go wrong?' with us and/or others and the world. In the experience of 'never enough' we become bottomless barrels, consuming products and services which will distance us from ourselves and each other further. This lack of trust in ourselves will not only clear the path to outcomes we would rather prevent but they also keep us from developing the political potential and awareness of our social environment, for which our time is calling.

The world is pregnant with a new story. I felt it when I was pregnant with my son. Pregnancy is not an illness. It is a celebration of life.

The growing life inside my body was sacred and there was a mutuality between me and my baby. We grew each other. We informed each other of the right choices in our 'mother tongue,' in a language older than words. I trusted the new life and consciousness coming into the world through me. It was (r)evolutionary.

Towards the end of my pregnancy I had several dreams in which my baby was talking with me and reassuring me that all was well despite all the fear-mongering going on around me. I had found a wonderful down-to-earth midwife whom I trusted and I had an undisturbed and powerful birthing experience at home. I was grateful for the calming presence of my partner, a friend, and my midwife. Presence was all I needed. I did not need intervention. I was in a space in which I felt safe and cared for.

In all my decisions I was guided by my intuition and my courage to follow it. This was against my cultural conditioning and especially against my training as a psychologist. "Trust is the most revolutionary political term that exists today." (Duhm, 2018)

Birthing requires a degree of trust and surrender which has been undermined by thousands of years of misogyny. The feminine life-giving wisdom has not been part of public, political or scientific life. Considering that every human being arrives on this earth through a female body, it would have served us well if we had paid a little more attention to the experience of women as they experience motherhood.

Women who are pregnant have the experience of being one and two at the same time; original systems thinkers who know that to care for self is to care for the other or to harm the other is to harm the self. To host the unfolding life of another human being inside the body is a unique feminine experience.

In our polarising world it is difficult to use the language of "feminine" and "masculine" and even harder to talk about "patriarchy", but we can no longer afford to cut out the life-giving, earth-based feminine wisdom which can lead us, men and women, away from the evolutionary dead end of the patriarchal domination system.

If we want to restore wholeness on this planet we need to re-integrate the wisdom of the feminine 'experience,' not 'ideas' about it. As Philip Shepherd writes: "Allegiance to ideas over experience is the essence and defining trait of patriarchy everywhere, and on all levels." (Shepherd, 2019)

Our general 'ideas' about pregnancy are to a large degree based on a scientific medical model which does not value women's 'experience.' How the pregnancy changes women's physical, mental and emotional processes is intelligent. Life is intelligent. Working against it is not.

I felt never more intelligent and powerful than when I was pregnant. Walking out of my obstetrician's office was one of many instances of being in touch with my feminine intelligence and power. I now look back on a parenting journey of 18 years. I can say that trusting this feminine intelligence helped me to always bring my attention back to my most important task: valuing myself in my role and worth as a mother. Following the truth of the trusting connection despite the many challenges we as conscious parents encounter in an unconscious and fear-driven environment is evolutionary activism. Now we, as parents, have to find the courage and the language to co-create the cultural conditions to trust the emerging power of our inter-connectedness.

Llewellyn Vaughan-Lee writes:

> Now is the time for this wisdom of the feminine to be combined with masculine consciousness, so that a new understanding of the wholeness of life can be used to help us to heal our world. Our present scientific solutions come from the masculine tools of analysis, the very mind set of separation that has caused the problems. We cannot afford to isolate ourself from the whole any more, and the fact that our problems are global illustrate this. Global warming is not just a scientific image but a dramatic reality. Combining masculine and feminine wisdom we can come to understand the relationships between the parts and the whole, and if we listen we can hear life telling us how to redress this imbalance. (Vaughan-Lee, 2009)

Because we have been living in this imbalance for generation after generation, misogyny has been normalised and with it the violation and destruction of life. As soon as we understand that misogyny is not the hatred of women but the hatred of life, we can and must work together as men and women, as mothers and fathers, in bringing an end to the war against ourselves and each other and heal the past and the future at the same time.

This is our 'Living Work' now: to reconnect with the feminine energy, says Kingsley Dennis:

> The current manifestation of feminine energy needs new pathways in order to enter and permeate our material world. Our physical structures are responding to this call by shifting from top-down structures to distributed and decentralised networks. Yet we also need to assist this recalibration by changing the ways we think. Altering the ways we do things will not gain permanence until human consciousness changes. In order to allow the new incoming consciousness to flow into the world, we need to allow it to flow through us. That is, to manifest the qualities, attitudes and our presence in the world that will most effectively receive, hold and transmit this consciousness." (Dennis, 2013)

In the *The Phoenix Generation* (2014) Dennis describes how a new generation is bringing in a new era of connection, compassion and consciousness while he sees our generation as the "bridging" generation.

As this bridging generation we are living between stories and are required to become 'bilingual.'

The language we have been speaking is the one of our globalised economic machine's language in which everything, including us, is viewed as commodity and as separate parts which can be bought and sold, fixed or replaced; to eventually be displaced by a 'better' version of humans, finally merging with the machine.

The other language which we are re-learning right now is our 'mother tongue,' the language of living systems which are self-directed, self-renewing and self-transcending and interconnected. A language of the living earth, of inter-being, which has been spoken by indigenous cultures all over the world.

The *Sixteen Indigenous Guiding Principles for Co-Creating a Sustainable, Harmonious, Prosperous World* published by the Four Worlds International Institute are one example of this kind of language.

In his recent essay 'The Language of the Master,' writer and "recovering environmentalist," Paul Kingsnorth asks: "If this language … has become a tool of control, what kind of language could be a tool to undo it? … Another way of framing that question: what languages does the Machine not speak?" (Kingsnorth, 2019)

The language the machine does not speak is love and trust.

To learn and practise this language with each other and our children we need to move beyond the habitual and institutional barriers which isolate us from each other and keep us trapped in harmful habits of highly individualised lives. We need to come together in self-organised small circles which break our isolation and allow us to meet in our real experience and not fight over outdated ideas of how life should be.

Co-creating compassionate spaces for ourselves and each other as parents is evolutionary activism. Our children will need our calming presence as much as they need to see us stand up for them and all life. They will be required to be healers and warriors at the same time; activists who fall in love with the earth and all life and passionately defend the sacred.

How do we do it?

Keep seeing the 'miracle' in them and every day celebrate being alive together by honouring the whole wild spectrum of human experience.

Charles Eisenstein gives a description of a miracle as an invitation for all of us to step into a larger world in which new things are possible:

> What is a miracle? It is not the intercession of a supernatural being into material affairs, not an event that violates the laws of the universe. A miracle is something that is impossible from one's current understanding of reality and truth but that becomes possible from a new understanding. (Eisenstein, 2009)

In her brilliant poem *Human Emergency*, Liv Torc (2019) faces the pain of bringing up her daughter in this time of global upheaval and her response to the paradox of the simultaneous breakup and breakthrough is believing and seeing the 'miracle' in her child. It ends with these words:

> *Isn't it better to say 'It's incredibly scary. It's as bad as they say.'*
> *But you are alive and you are a miracle,*
> *and that has to mean something.*
> *And it's you who might be standing at the moment where everything ends.*
> *But your generation has the power to save the whole world.*
> *And I'm gonna help you because I've got your back.*
> *And I am a miracle too.*
> *And guess what?*
> *There is something out there more courageous and potent than science and I believe it will help us because*
> *I've touched it and felt it and*
> *I've seen it.*
> *In you.*

References

Dennis, K 2013, 'The Living Work: Reconnecting with the Feminine Energy,' *HuffPost*, 23 January.

Dennis, K 2014, *The Phoenix Generation*, Watkins Publishing, London.

Duhm, D 2018, 'Dieter Duhm,' *tamera*, <https://www.tamera.org/dieter-duhm>.

Eisenstein, C 2009, 'In the Miracle,' *charleseisenstein.org*, <https://charleseisenstein.org/essays/in-the-miracle/>.

Eisenstein, C 2013, 'The Space between Stories,' *charleseisenstein.org*, <https://charleseisenstein.org/essays/2013-the-space-between-stories/>.

Holt, J 1983, *How Children Learn*, 2nd edn, Delacorte Press, New York. (Reprinted by Perseus Press 1995)

Kingsnorth, P 2019, The Language of the Master,' *emergence magazine*, <https://emergencemagazine.org/story/the-language-of-the-master/>.

Korten, D 2007, 'The Great Turning: From Empire to Earth Community,' *davidkorten.org*, <https://davidkorten.org/great-turning-book/>.

Lane, P 2019, *Sixteen Indigenous Guiding Principles for Co-Creating a Sustainable, Harmonious, Prosperous World*, Four Worlds International Institute,<https://www.fwii.net/profiles/blogs/sixteen-guiding-principles-for>.

Macy, J 2012 & 2014, *The Great Turning*, <https://www.activehope.info/great-turning.html (2012)>; <http://www.joannamacyfilm.org/ (2014)>.

Shepherd, P 2019, *Radical Wholeness*, Omega, <https://philipshepherd.com/omega/>.

Torc, L 2019, 'The Human Emergency,' *YouTube*, <https://www.youtube.com/watch?v=9-IuL-ks048>.

Vaughan-Lee, L 2009, *The Return of the Feminine and the World Soul*, Golden Sufi Center, Point Reyes Station, California.

7

The future of intelligence

Dr Ricci-Jane Adams

I RECALL THE FEELING of the wash of amniotic fluid rush around me on the bed as the young doctor leaned forward between my tented legs to break my waters. So much fluid for a baby who is two weeks overdue, I thought to myself. There wasn't time for much more quiet thought after that. The doctor looked up at me with something akin to terror in her eyes. It was not what I wanted to see. The midwife in the room exchanged some terse words with the young doctor, still hovering between my legs. All I remember hearing was *cord prolapse*. I knew what that meant. Like many first time mothers I had spent my pregnancy reading everything I could on being pregnant, and on what could go wrong.

Umbilical **cord prolapse** is a complication that occurs prior to or during delivery of the baby. In a **prolapse**, the umbilical **cord** drops (prolapses) through the open cervix into the vagina ahead of the baby. The **cord** can then become trapped against the baby's body during delivery. It results in lack of oxygen to the baby. The consequences of that don't need to be spelt out. In medical jargon, the resulting action is called a 'crash caesar' — the most emergency of all emergency caesars. In other words, get the baby out immediately.

Someone hit the button on the wall or made the call. Throughout the hospital the emergency was declared. Within moments it seemed the small room was choked with medical staff. I knew I was supposed to get onto my hands and knees and to take pressure off the cord, to try and free up the oxygen supply to my unborn baby. Someone got me into this position, a doctor on the gurney behind me, pushing the head away from the cord. Within minutes I was several floors up in the hospital operating theatre looking into the face of the anaesthetist as he counted down from ten. The last thing I heard was a doctor yelling, *we have to get this baby out of her*. Then everything went black. My first born son was brought into the world seven minutes after my waters were broken.

Perhaps his birth was the portend I should have heeded. Everything about my son's life from his arrival in this world, onwards, has been different to my expectations. I don't know if my son's neurodiversity is as a direct result of his birth, although the evidence indicates this is so, but I do know that he and I have never had the luxury of privileging ordinary ideas of intelligence, and how we make meaning of the world. My son understands 'differently,' and this has been one of the greatest blessings to support me to see differently too. It has led to my life's work, as I watched my creative, empathic and highly intuitive child struggle with a world ruled by intellect.

It is time to change our minds about what constitutes intelligence. It is time to change the conversation about our highest form of intelligence — intuition. It is my life's work to mainstream the intuitive sciences so we can reclaim our intuitive intelligence. To future-proof our children, and to support them to positively embrace, and effectively handle whatever comes next, it is inevitable that we need to consider other forms of intelligence. I have witnessed this first hand for my son for whom ordinary ideas of intelligence have been the reason for his consistent exclusion.

For intelligent, educated people in the West, intuition has, however, been considered a fabrication of magical thinking — evidence of a mental health issue at worst and *woo-woo* culture at best. It is not easy to talk about our non-dominant senses with a mainstream audience, even though for more than 100 years quantum physicists have been explaining the vibrational truth of the Universe, which is the very reason intuitive intelligence functions.

My task in this essay is to: provide evidence of the existence and potency of a form of intelligence that we all have access to, and that I believe has the capacity to support our children to thrive in the current/coming time of uncertainty and chaos; and to offer simple, applied techniques that we can utilise, share with our children, and integrate into the fabric of daily lives. I also share the inevitable legacy of the development of this kind of non-dominant intelligence, which has a direct impact on the way our story as a collective unfolds.

Is there a way to have a conversation about intuition that goes beyond the New Age ghetto, and beyond spiritual trinkets and superstitions (the crystals, oracle cards and unverified healing modalities) that will support our children to see their own brilliance outside of the IQ scale? When we look to the science, there is. Our innate ability to understand and connect with one another beyond the dominant five senses — in other words to activate our intuitive intelligence — is premised on our very biology in two ways:

1 Intuitive intelligence is an intelligence based on the inherent interconnectedness of all consciousness, and our capacity to attune to that unified nonlocal and a-causal consciousness with focused intention and attention. We produce electro-magnetic fields made up of vibrating particles that are in communication with everything around us beyond the limits of our physical because of this fact.

2 We have a little brain in our heart, which sends more information to the brain than the other way around. Intuitive intelligence is a function of the heart brain, a cluster of 40,000 neural cells in the anatomical heart that has been demonstrated to be precognisant, and with an electro-magnetic field 500 times greater than the cranial brain.

As a result of these two biological premises, we have access to intuitive intelligence, which simultaneously contributes to a sense of self-reliance and to a deep sense of connection to others. How is that so? Let's look to the science.

At the quantum level, subatomic particles are ripples in an electro-magnetic field. The ripples create those fields. So subatomic particles, which are not particles but waves of motion, move in a field. Everything, from the subatomic particle to the entire universe generates a field. We are fields, within fields, within fields. These fields of motion influence everything around us. Our field is influencing the field of the Universe, as well as the field of the person next to us. We know that there is a unified field connecting everything. We can learn to actively connect with this nonlocal field to guide our lives and have access to the information we need in any moment.

We do this by learning to privilege our heart brain. Our heart is the communication portal to the quantum field because it generates the largest electro-magnetic field of any part of the human body. The heart is so much more than a muscle that pumps blood.

When a new life is conceived in utero, something remarkable happens around day 17 of gestation. Into the primitive kidney bean shape of the new life forming, down the primitive space that will become the throat, a cluster of cells appears from somewhere in the womb. Science does not know from whence these cells come.

This small cluster of cells moves into the primitive branches of what will become the lungs and the heartbeat begins. Quite literally, the substance of the heart is a scientific mystery. Its beginnings are of a mystical origin.

The heart is the bridge between the local and nonlocal fields. It possesses a profound and undervalued form of intelligence. It is this form of intelligence that ensures children like my son are not left disconnected from themselves and the world around them because they do not fit the dominant mould of intelligence.

In a study by HeartMath Institute's psychophysiologist Rollin McCraty in 2004, it was found that a participant's heart rate significantly slowed before a future emotional picture was shown to them; that while both the heart and brain receive and respond to intuitive information, the heart appears to receive that information first. What the HeartMath studies suggest is that the heart is the main conduit that connects us to the quantum field, and that it is the heart that then relays intuitive information to the brain.

Raymond Bradley explains the action of nonlocal intuition or intuitive intelligence in the following way. His theory is born of experiments designed to understand the success of repeat entrepreneurs. His study (2007) explains how the entrepreneur's passionately focused attention directed to an object of interest (e.g., a future business opportunity) attunes the bio-emotional energy generated by the body's psychophysiological systems to a domain of quantum-holographical information, which contains implicit, energetically-encoded information.

In layman's terms, what this means is that when we focus our feeling state, we tune into a domain beyond the world of the senses, described here as 'quantum-holographic information,' that contains information that is energetically encoded.

I recall a night several years ago when my son, now 12-years-old, was terribly out of sorts. He was oppositional and angry and rejecting all forms of attention and love. Eventually, as he crawled in to bed he said to me, "I'm sad because something is wrong with Ebony."

Ebony, his little sister, who lived across town with their dad and step-mother, had just been admitted to hospital with a severe infection of the salivary glands that caused her face and neck to swell and triggered a great deal of pain. Back at our house we weren't yet privy to that information. But my son knew something was up. To console him I sent his dad a message and didn't think about it again.

The next morning we found out that my son was, of course, right to be concerned. Ebony fully recovered, but this direct experience of my son's intuition left me deeply contemplative about the inherent interconnectedness of all consciousness. My son's love for his sister (passionately-focused attention) gave him access to knowledge about his sister non-locally (quantum-holographical information) that had not yet been shared with us locally.

What was happening here? And can this innate intelligence that my son was demonstrating be cultivated and educated in the same way as any other form of intelligence from intellect to emotion? It is my experience that the answer is *yes*.

How do we bring this all together? The key to living in an intuitively intelligent state is what I call Congruence. This practice is built on the science of coherence developed by HeartMath Institute. We are incongruent when the logical brain, usually through feelings of stress, ignores or resists the intuitive intelligence that emerges from the heart brain. Congruence is created through generating positive feeling states. When we move into a congruent state, the heart and brain act together. This is exactly what we need to occur to make our intuitive intelligence clear and accurate. The mind must bow to the intuitive intelligence of the heart. We alter the electric and magnetic fields of the atom by changing our emotions.

There is a very simple practice we can use at anytime and teach our children that switches on our intuitive intelligence.

Here's the process:

First, close the eyes or simply turn your attention inwards, away from the outer world of local reality.

Extend the breath to the count of four on the inward breath and six on the out breath (diaphragmatic breathing activates our parasympathetic nervous system moving us out of a stress response).

Continue this for a few breaths. Then, adjust this to your own comfortable rhythm.

Take two fingers or your palm to the centre of your chest and lightly touch this part of your body. Here, we are bringing our consciousness to this part of physiology, inviting our mind to follow.

Now, turn all your thoughts to a single memory or a moment that inspires positive feeling states. Or make a mental list of all the things for which you feel gratitude from the last 24 hours of your life. No matter how small, the idea is to really feel the feelings of gratitude, freedom and joy.

Let yourself be consumed by these feelings. Do this for at least three minutes (you'll perhaps observe that this feels like a really long time at first!).

It may feel as though there is a field of energy surrounding your heart area that is expanding the longer you stay in this practice. Imagine, feel or sense that field and notice that sense of expansion.

Gently lower your hand to your lap and let go of the practice. When you are ready open your eyes and go about your day.

The aim of this practice is to maintain that state of congruence ultimately at all times. In the day-to-day of raising our children, and supporting them and ourselves with the tsunami of emotions we encounter even just in the ordinary activities of our lives, this practice is a refuge from the chaos, the noise and the doubt.

Congruence is also the precursor to our intuitive intelligence. We can be clear connection with this form of intelligence when we privilege staying congruent. We can live a life typified by intuitive intelligence.

So, if that is the case, what does intuitive intelligence feel like? How can we know when we are in an intuitively intelligent state of being? And, what are the qualities of living from our intuitive intelligence? I have come to know the power of these qualities well by offering (and failing to offer!) them to my own children.

The Qualities of an Intuitively Intelligent Life

There are several key qualities of intuitive intelligence. As adults, most of us have been educated 'out' of a natural relationship to these qualities, so we have to relearn intuitive intelligence. We can ensure for our children that this disconnection never occurs.

As parents, we can build an ecosystem around our children that naturally supports them to remain deeply rooted in their intuitive wisdom by applying these qualities. And in so doing we can build our own long neglected intuitive muscle.

So what are the qualities of intuitive intelligence, and the conditions in which intuitive intelligence flourishes?

Presence

In creating an ecology for the natural development of our child's intuitive intelligence there must be *presence*. A life full of rushing and structured activity does not permit the child to expand into full presence in this moment now. When we rush our toddlers from the car seat to the café back to the car to the playgroup, feeling stress and urgency in every moment we are not present. Presence means allowing each moment to guide us to the best course of action.

When we allow our children and ourselves to be present we are tuning in to what we are feeling bodily, emotionally and energetically. Without that we can tend to overtax the nervous system and live in our sympathetic nervous system response — fight, flight or freeze — even when we are not in a life threatening situation. Stress reduces our capacity to connect to our intuitive intelligence. The high beta brainwave state that we are in when we are in our sympathetic nervous system closes off the communication between the heart brain and the cranial brain. We can begin practicing presence just by slowing down, scheduling less, and practicing the technique of Coherence, which powerfully brings us back to the present moment.

Trust

Trusting our children sounds deceptively simple, but what if it means cancelling plans, or changing direction or letting go of our idea of what should happen? I am not advocating a boundary-less and chaotic home, but rather a willingness to listen deeply to the intuitive intelligence of our child. This requires us to also trust ourselves, of course. The cultivation of trust of our children and ourselves means that we are willing to disappoint others, to risk letting people down. Not going to that birthday party or family gathering, for example, when it is clear that your child needs to stay quietly in his imaginative play. To intuitively privilege the needs of our children, and often the needs of ourselves, builds courage within us. We learn to listen to ourselves, and withdraw our worth from external validation.

Self-worth

The upshot of trusting your child is that of course he or she develops a robust sense of self-worth. It can't be any other way. Every time a child is truly witnessed she is affirmed from within. When self-worth is nourished in the very tiny child that worthiness is remarkably unbreakable, through all of life's uncertainty and challenges.

To cultivate that worthiness we need to be responsive to the child. That means many things, but trusting them is a huge part of a developing intuition. This trust is as simple as picking up the baby when it is crying or cancelling plans if your toddler is clearly demanding a day at home. Every time we take this action of responding to our child, intuitively, we affirm the child deep down within them in a way that gives the unshakeable faith in themselves. And then they don't need a single thing outside of themselves to know their own worth.

Imagination

Imagination is the gateway to intuitive intelligence — expressed through symbol, feeling, image, and creative inspiration. It is a non-dominant form of intelligence and is easy to miss if we do not learn how to connect with it. When we suspend reason and analysis we enter into the realm of intuitive intelligence. For the child, who resides effortlessly in the realm of imagination, there is nothing that needs to be understood here. They are imaginative, creative geniuses, often until they are educated out of it. It is our role as the parent to permit the cultivation of the imaginative skill simply by getting out of the way. Over-structuring the child's daily life with organised tasks, activities and constant rushing about (sense a theme here?), will remove the child from his or her natural imaginative power. As we value the imagination in the child, the child retains connection to his or her intuitive intelligence as they grow, and without any effort, are able to stay aware of the communication from this more subtle intelligence.

The child raised to know her intuitive intelligence trusts her creative inspiration, the big ideas that arrive into her consciousness, and has the courage to take action on them. A young teenager called Greta Thunberg stunned the world in 2018 when she demanded that the world leader's panic about the state of climate change. "If I didn't have Asperger's and wasn't so strange I would be stuck in this social game that everyone else seems to be so infatuated with … It makes me function a bit differently … I see the world differently," Greta said in a television interview in 2019. This difference in perception is born of trusting what emerges from within us, from our inspiration, and it can be protected and inspired in our children when we let them lead from their imagination. We contribute to a generation of self-approving, original thinkers.

The result of an activated intuitive intelligence is that we no longer believe we are separate and isolated. We experience oneness as a natural and true state. We are in total flow with life. For the child, this state of flow is what they are innately, and when we create an ecology that supports feelings of presence, trust, self-worth, imagination and privileging the wisdom of the heart over the head, we are contributing to that intuitively intelligent child becoming an intuitively intelligent adult.

What it leads to is a sense of personal reliance, personal responsibility, and personal empowerment. If indeed it is true that I am a field within the fields of everything around me, then I have the capacity to positively influence my world just by cultivating a different feeling state. This truth inevitably leads to a greater sense of connection to contributing something to the greater good.

This is what I call *spiritual activism*.

Spiritual Activism

What differentiates social activism from spiritual activism? Is spiritual activism just social activism done by spiritual people? No. Spiritual activism is informed by the shift in perception that happens when we have a made a conscious commitment to live with the awareness of our inherent inter-connectedness.

The recognition that we are not isolated and separate, through the use of such practices as Congruence, opens us to the deeper purpose of our lives, which is not personal gain but collective good.

As we pursue the path of intuitive intelligence, then we must be prepared for the reality that the things we desire will change. It is inevitable because we are shifting daily away from the Newtonian view of reality into our heart's intelligence. We want to serve the greater good before all else. Our life becomes one of sacred service. Inevitably, our life becomes one of spiritual activism, too, for sacred service and spiritual activism are one. All those who have connected to their heart's intuitive intelligence will move from an individual identity to a collective, community based identity. This is spiritual activism in action. Our inner work pours out of us into the world, and we yearn to make a shift for all, for we know, *I am that*. It's science.

The inevitable end point of the development of our intuitive intelligence is a permanent shift in perception. The shift in perception from the idea of intuitive intelligence being an external thing we are seeking, to the activation of an internal state of being is the shift to living with intuitive intelligence. We don't just 'tap into' our intuition when we want to answer a question. Instead, we *live* our intuitive intelligence, we trust it, and we act upon our intuitive intelligence without doubt. This is intuition beyond the trinkets and superstitions of the New Age. We need nothing outside of ourselves. Because we have changed our minds about what we are, we now understand what we have. This is the end of separation thinking and the most radical form of service to the world that I believe we can take.

When we raise our children to know how to connect to their highest form of intelligence, so that they know inherent interconnectedness as their truth, they have a sense of belonging, self-trust, self-worth, are attuned effortlessly to the more subtle communication of their imagination, we have equipped them with everything they need to both thrive in uncertainty, and to create a new paradigm for all. The challenge for us as the adult care-givers is to put down our cynicism and perhaps even our prejudice in regards to non-dominant intelligence, and open to the possibility of a bigger picture we are capable of and what we can offer the world at this extraordinary time.

References

Bradley, R *et al* 2007, 'Nonlocal Intuition in Entrepreneurs and Non-entrepreneurs: An Experimental Comparison Using Electrophysiological Measures,' *World Futures: Journal of General Evolution*, 23 January, <noosphere.princeton.edu/papers/pdf/bradley.intuition.2007.pdf>.

McCraty, R 2004, 'The Grateful Heart: The Psychophysiology of Appreciation,' *HeartMath.org*, <https://www.heartmath.org/research/research-library/basic/grateful-heart-the-psychophysiology-of-appreciation>.

Sacred activism and being an ally

Phoebe Mwanza

WE LIVE IN A BEAUTIFUL and abundant world. It is such a privilege and an honour to be a part of it, and to have the opportunity to raise a family in it. However, there are people who do not always share in this abundance and whose experiences in this world are not as beautiful, just and fair. This may be because of historical reasons that continue to cause ongoing systemic issues and disadvantage. It may be because wealth is not always distributed equally. It could also be because of social, economic or political disadvantage, discrimination, racism or poverty. Whatever the reason, it leads us to situations where our fellow human's experiences on earth leave a lot to be desired.

As parents, it is important that we are cognisant of the world in which our children are being raised, the interactions they have and the connections that they form. It is our responsibility to ensure that our children play their part in creating a better world for other children and future generations.

From a spiritual perspective, if we are all connected and are part of a universal consciousness, seeing one of our brothers and sisters suffer[1] should prompt us to speak up for those who are unable or do not have the platforms or the resources to do so. It should galvanise us to take action to ensure that every person has equal access to wealth, opportunity, resources, education, health services and employment opportunities to ensure we are truly living our life to the fullest. It is also important to not only build a better future for all our children — biological or not — but to model our actions to younger generations.

The experience of oneness and unity consciousness should not be an abstract concept or experience that only occurs outside of this physical reality. Instead, universal and unity consciousness should be firmly rooted into our physical reality.

A person who is consciously on a spiritual journey should be empowered to be an activist, a sacred activist, because seeing the sacredness and divinity in each other should fuel us to want the best for one another. This level of consciousness and understanding flows down to our children, helping them to be empowered to be activists in their own right.

Activism is when a person dedicates their energy, resources, time, money, platform and life to highlight causes that are close to their heart, including the injustices that other groups of people experience. They dedicate their lives to improving the lives of people around them who continue to experience discrimination, oppression, injustice and poverty. Sacred activism is activism that is fuelled from a form of spirituality. It is deeply rooted in love — love of oneself and love for our fellow humans.

An example is the American civil rights leader, Dr Martin Luther King who was a Baptist minister and a founder of the Southern Christian Leadership Conference, a group of religious leaders who risked their lives for civil rights in the 1950s and 1960s. Malcolm X, also known as Malik el-Shabazz, a Muslim Minister and a human rights activist, was another prominent figure in the civil rights movement. He was instrumental in bringing to the forefront the plight of African Americans. Both their spiritual beliefs and their deep love for humanity, and especially the members of their community who were facing vast inequality, segregation and discrimination at the time, motivated them to act and become activists, leaders and spokespersons in their country.

Why is spirituality an important part of sacred activism?

An activist — and particularly one who is a parent — without a spiritual base can potentially do more harm than good. Being a sacred activist helps us to become better people, and subsequently raise better people. This is because a sacred activist is always seeking to become a better person. They are dedicated to personal transformation as they realise that this is an integral part of the process of creating massive external transformation that creates a better world. It is not enough to change the external world without changing our own world first. As Mahatma Ghandi once said: *"Be the change, you wish to see in the world."* A parent who is continually seeking personal growth and transformation models this behaviour to their children.

Sacred activists recognise that the change in the world starts within themselves before they ever go out into the world. As sacred activists, we seek to heal and change ourselves first through a total physical, spiritual and emotional transformation before seeking to heal and change others. This is the only way we can create a complete transformation of the world around us.

This is a recognition that there is no good that comes from us being dedicated activists and parents trying to create a better world for others and for the planet when we still go home at the end of the day and engage in toxic behaviour, replicate oppressive patterns in personal relationships and do not practice love, compassion, or forgiveness to the people in our own lives. Like my therapist once said: "Beware the dragon slayer does not become the dragon." This was in reference to how in my life I was working as a human rights lawyer who was dedicated to changing laws and policies to ensure everyone was treated equally yet, in my own home, I engaged in very toxic and unhealthy behaviour with my now ex-husband. I did not practice patience, empathy, kindness and understanding — which is what I was essentially asking from the rest of the world in my work.

In addition, I view sacred activism as an expression of love. Helping another becomes a form of self-love as well as an expression of outward love, because we can not love our fellow human without first having experienced loving ourselves. Che Guevara, a major figure in the Cuban revolution, once said:

> The true revolutionary is guided by a great feeling of love. It is impossible to think of a genuine revolutionary lacking this quality. (Guevara, 1965)

The sacred activist is therefore guided by a deep feeling of love towards their children and other fellow humans. This love permeates their actions, their words and how they choose to show up for others.

Activism can be physically and emotionally draining. It is draining to constantly see the effects of injustice. Witnessing poverty, discrimination, oppression, abuse and injustices over and over can be draining and cause burn out. Of course witnessing these experiences does not compare to actually living through these experiences. However, having daily spiritual practices can help provide a healing, refuelling and a safe haven when we need to take time out from the activist's work. These practices can be in the form of, for example: meditation, a yoga practice, spending time in nature, prayer, self love practices, practicing moon rituals, and self-healing, which can all be taught to and shared with children.

Activism that comes from a sacred place ensures that every decision we make and the steps we take in this space do not cause more harm. It ensures that we do not inadvertently cause more oppression or replicate the very systems we are seeking to transform. We have more empathy, understanding and patience which ensures that our actions have integrity, are honourable and are consequently transformative.

Why should spiritual people be activists?

It is my view that anyone on a conscious spiritual journey is fully aware of how all human beings, no matter their age, gender or background, are connected. That recognition in itself should be enough to galvanise a person to ensure that, no matter how small or big their actions are, everyone is having a full and abundant experience whilst here in this physical reality for the following reasons:

- The fact that we are all connected and interconnected should be a motivator for anyone on a spiritual journey to want a major, radical, transformative change on all levels of life. This includes advocating for huge social, economic or political change across the world. Our children and fellow humans are a part of us and when they suffer and when the earth is suffering, then we all suffer as well because we are all connected. Our individual enlightenment cannot be achieved without universal enlightenment. If we believe that we are truly connected and interconnected, then we know that our individual spiritual growth and enlightenment is dependent upon the growth and transformation of the collective. This is why we have to do our part to contribute to alleviating the injustices others face.

- The height of spiritual enlightenment is being of service to others. All the prominent people who had a profound effect on humanity or changed the course of humanity spent most of their lives in service to others. A selfish spirituality that is only concerned with one's own personal transformation, needs and wants has never boded well with me.

- We want to create a new world based on the wisdom and teachings of loving strangers, justice for all, compassion, empathy, kindness and experiencing the grandeur and abundance of the universe. This new world we wish to create will need to be based on new paradigms of love, acceptance, empathy, and compassion — the opposite of our current world. This requires the sacred activist to walk in the basic tenets of spirituality including love, empathy, and compassion, and to pass these on to the next generations.

- There are many people who have reincarnated across the world with the sole purpose of helping to radically transform the world we live in. They are here to contribute to the healing and ascension of the planet and its inhabitants. They are sometimes referred to as *lightworkers*. Lightworkers come in all shapes and forms. They can be lawyers. They can be politicians. They can be doctors. They can be engineers. They can be teachers. They can be parents. They are our children. Lightworkers have to do the work that dismantles the very systems that continue to oppress our fellow brothers and sisters. The work that needs to be done is the kind that completely destroys and transforms the social, economic and political systems that we have at the moment. These systems are patriarchal or based on a system of white supremacy that continues to fuel injustices across the world. The world needs more people who are going to revolutionise these systems and lead from a spiritual base and be the new business leaders, political leaders, teachers, police force, lawyers or judges. Every fabric of our society needs to be revolutionised. Whatever we choose to do, we can use our influence, starting with our own families, work, community and platform to completely transform our society.

How to be a sacred activist

Sacred activism requires that:

- All action should be based on the motivating emotions of love and compassion. We must always seek what we have in common with others, rather than what divides us. We are all connected through our shared humanity. When we view each other through our connectedness, it is easier to lead from a place of love. When we approach our work this way, our actions shift from helping others to helping for the benefit of the collective.

- We set our ego aside and work with others whenever possible. It is not important or necessary that we receive credit for our work or that we are the face of our cause. It is more important that we come together and find long lasting solutions that help to heal and transform the world. The ego has no place here.

- We do all things with honesty and integrity. The end does not justify the means in this space. All the actions we take, all the decisions we make and all the energy we send out when doing this work is important. This is how the new world will be created — with foundations of love and integrity. This is how the transformation will last the distance.

- We search for solutions that are holistic and sustainable. We have to think about the generations that are coming after us through the way we look after our planet. We have to co-create with our natural environment. Any action we take in this space should be done with a deep respect, love and understanding of our natural environment. We also have to think about the world we want our children to live in and the legacies we want to leave behind through how our social, economic and political structures are designed. Any solutions we seek must ensure that the dignity of individual humans and their communities are restored or maintained and that the earth does not continue to suffer.

- We respect the history, traditions, cultures and wisdom that Indigenous groups continue to hold. These groups hold ancient wisdoms that can help us with the solutions to transform our environment and our social, political and economic systems. We should teach our children our true history and about the strength, resilience and wisdom that our Indigenous brothers and sisters hold.

- We become allies and co-conspirators to groups of people that continue to face injustices, oppression and discrimination such as Indigenous people, black people or other people of colour.

I want to spend more time on the last point in particular because it is an opportunity to really show up for groups that continue to experience marginalisation, oppression and discrimination. How we *show up* as allies can do a lot of good and really transform peoples lives. However, we can also potentially do more harm than good if we are not mindful of how we do this. Below are some tips on how to be an effective and unproblematic ally, which can also be shared with children in an age-appropriate manner.

How to be an ally

Indigenous people, black people and people of colour disproportionately experience marginalisation, discrimination and oppression in comparison to other groups.[2] As a sacred activist, being an ally to people of colour is an important and effective aspect of being an activist. However, it involves a lot of self-reflection, education, and listening. It means knowing and understanding that we are often coming from a position of power and privilege.

This privilege has been gained through unjust systems that marginalise the groups that you are seeking to be ally for. It's not enough to show up in solidarity and speak out against these unjust systems; we have to do what is within our power to dismantle these systems. We also need to change our own behaviours and be mindful that we are not contributing to keeping these systems going. If we are not mindful, our children may pick up on our behaviours and continue the same behaviours.

Below are some things to consider when being an ally to people of colour:

Do not speak for people of colour Being an ally involves recognising that these groups of people have spent decades, and sometimes centuries, not being able to speak up for themselves or express themselves for fear of persecution. So when they do, it's important that we do not continue to repress their voices. Doing so can be harmful as it presumes that they do not have the intellectual capacity and knowledge to express their own views and needs. It inadvertently causes harm by continuing the oppression that made them cease to speak in the first place. No matter how well intentioned speaking up for them feels like, it is important that we instead build people's capacity to speak up for themselves and encourage our children to do the same.

In the alternative, it is important that we seek permission to speak for them and to tell their stories as told to us, not our version of their stories. People of colour have voices and they are not afraid to use them. There are many people who work closely with these groups of people and are highly educated in topics relating to issues affecting them. Problems can arise when people of colour are the minority group in a country which can lead to the majority groups dominating the conversations in these areas.

True self-determination[3] means supporting these groups and working with them, but also allowing them to speak on the subjects that have an impact on their lives. If we are true allies, then we will not mind doing the work behind the scenes without any of the glory. So, this may look like saying no to the radio or television interview and recommending a person of colour instead or recommending consulting a person of colour when something we are working on touches an area that may have tremendous affect on them.

In addition, when people of colour speak up it is important that we do not dictate, talk over, or suppress their voices. We have to be okay with not being included in all conversations concerning them. It is also important that we do not 'whitesplain.' This is a term used when a non person of colour explains topics regarding race, injustice and inequality to a people of colour, often in an obliviously condescending manner. It is essentially an expression of privilege and paternalism.

Whitesplaining usually happens when a person of colour complains about racism, and someone comments with phrases such as "You always see race," or "You are too emotional" and proceeds to re-imagine, re-tell or explain away the experiences of that person. It essentially dismisses their experience. It is like trying to tell a pilot how to land a plane or a surgeon how to perform surgery. It is important that we do not speak over people of colour or explain away their experiences. It comes across as condescending and will often be inaccurate or oversimplified. It also recreates and replicates the same systems that caused their silence in the first place. An ally's role is never to speak for others, but to take down the obstacles preventing them from speaking up for themselves.

Speak up for people of colour Although it may seem contrary to the point above, it is important for us to speak up for people of colour in certain circumstances. For example, when we are in rooms where they are not present and conversations or decisions are happening that affect them. Something as simple as highlighting the fact that a certain group of people need to be invited into the conversation can go a long way. This gesture could have prevented many organisations from making decisions leading to appropriation and insensitive marketing and design choices. An ally's role is to highlight that the conversation happening is problematic and may be offensive, insensitive or potentially discriminatory. It is also to ensure that a person of colour is invited into the room when certain decisions are being made.

It is important that we use our privilege and platforms to speak up regularly against the issues that arise because of the legacies of institutions such as slavery and colonialism. If you have a following or are in a position of authority, use it to illuminate these issues and more importantly, pass the mic on to us.

An ally's role is to speak up even when it's uncomfortable. We have to stand up to our racist family members, friends and colleagues when they are engaging in problematic conversations and behaviours. For example, if you hear racist slurs, someone reinforcing stereotypes, a person being dismissive about people of colour and their culture or someone engaging in 'micro-aggressions,'[4] then say something. Not saying anything condones their attitudes.

Allies usually have the advantage of being able to communicate more with, and being listened to more by, people from their own circle. This gives them a chance to help people of colour by promoting equality and justice, breaking down stereotypes and educating their own circle. It is important to do so even when there are no people of colour present to be offended. It is not always easy to be confrontational, but if you are a true ally, you will have to push past that discomfort. Your discomfort pales in comparison to what people of colour face on a regular basis. When we always speak up against injustice, no matter the audience, our children see this and model this behaviour.

Educate yourself   Our job as allies is to educate ourselves on the systems that are in place presenting challenges and barriers to people of colour. It should not always be the role of the person of colour in our circle of friends or in the workplace to constantly highlight the history, the nuances or the sensitivities of issues affecting them. It is our job to educate ourselves and our children.

Of course it goes without saying that when in doubt, we should ask the people of colour in our lives to ensure we are adequately informed. When doing this, we should be mindful of handling this with care because not all people of colour are comfortable being spokespeople for the rest of their group. Honestly, they shouldn't have to be. Non people of colour are afforded the luxury of individuality, while people of colour are usually lumped into groups when speaking on their experiences. It's not fair to shoulder the burden of speaking for an entire group on one person. The person may feel that if they speak up they will be ostracised or viewed as troublemakers — which is historically how people of colour have been viewed and treated when speaking up on issues affecting them.

So if we expect them to speak up on certain issues then we should create a safe space for them and protect them when the need arises. Always looking to the person of colour in our lives to be the expert on racism and to depend on them for advice on when racist words, behaviours or policies are at play is problematic and exhausting. Many of the issues people of colour face are not of their own making. We may not be responsible for instituting these systems but we either continue to uphold them, directly or indirectly, or benefit from them. It is our job as allies to take responsibility and accountability for educating ourselves and our children.

Create a safe space for people of colour to speak up   Continuing on from the above, people of colour are not always comfortable about speaking out because they fear losing their jobs or being ostracised socially. They have likely faced similar scenarios before. We can create spaces for them to speak up in situations where they are outnumbered, which is likely if they are the minority in the society. It is important that we co-sign, validate and support people of colour when they raise issues publicly because it takes a lot to speak up.

If we have the resources and power to do so then we should help create physical, digital or intellectual spaces and platforms for people of colour. When you do so, do not then proceed to dominate the same space that would be better filled by them. Help open up spaces without taking them over. Do not start a person of colour initiative without hiring or consulting any people of colour. It is great for non people of colour to help organise protests and create safe spaces for people of colour, but it is not good to then have their own voices centred and elevated over the voices of people of colour.

White saviour complex People of colour do not need to be 'saved.' They need non people of colour to be conscious of the systems in place that create barriers for them. The white saviour complex is another expression of white supremacy because it is rooted in the belief that a person's ideas and solutions are superior than that of a non person of colour because of their racial background. This person believes they have the answers to the challenges people of colour face and cannot fathom any alternatives outside of their own.

Because of historical, systematic and institutionalised power structures that span hundreds of years, the white saviour complex is problematic because it is a symptom of white supremacy and something we all have to work together to deconstruct. It propagates the attitude that non-people of colour know best and are therefore best placed to fix other peoples problems. There is room for genuine help that does not require documenting, selfie-taking or hashtagging good deeds. Doing this trivialises people's problems, oversimplifies systemic issues, exoticises communities and perpetuates tired and unhelpful stereotypes of certain groups. A sacred activist is cognisant that their role is not to 'fix' communities of colour but to learn and understand what communities need and work with them to achieve it.

Listen to people of colour Listening to people of colour is important. We have to listen without needing to provide solutions to their problems. We have to listen to understand. We have to listen in an authentic manner. When we listen and hear them, we realise they most likely have the answers to the challenges they face. Our role is to listen to, assist and facilitate the solutions that we have come up with. Never assume that you have enough information or experience to march ahead without stopping to check with a person of colour that you are heading in the right direction.

Help dismantle white supremacy White supremacy is a social, economic and political system and structure that oppresses and disadvantages people of colour. Our role as allies is to break down these systems and ensure full economic, social and political participation of people of colour. This includes helping to elect candidates of colour to ensure representation at all levels of government. It also includes ensuring that they are hired and promoted in the workplace in a fair manner and not overlooked because of their cultural backgrounds, their names or their accents. This means treating them as individuals and looks like including them in the social fabric of society whether in marketing campaigns or in the media we consume.

Work through shame and guilt and discomfort When working in this space it is very common for shame, guilt and discomfort to rise to the surface. This happens when realising the atrocities that your ancestors have committed to people of colour whose consequences continue to be felt. However, sharing this shame and guilt with people of colour is not particularly useful because it has the effect of either turning the spotlight back on you or, much worse, silencing them out of not wanting to hurt your feelings. When this happens, the person of colour is either silenced or they have to lower their voice or restate their views. If they do not do so, then they are viewed as being insensitive.

If non people of colour who are activists feel uncomfortable, it means that there cannot be a full and frank discussion of topics such as race and there can be no challenge to their privilege, which means no challenge to their power. It is our job as allies to work through our own guilt and shame without transferring it on to people of colour.

Be there for the good times and the bad A good ally will stand with people of colour at all times, not just when it is easy. This requires taking an active interest in our issues instead of romanticising certain aspects of people of colour's cultures. People of colour do not have the option of picking and choosing when to be people of colour. There is no button they can turn on and off. Allies need to stand with them, especially when the going gets rough. This means sustaining your engagement over time, not only when it is trendy. It also means learning about the ways people of colour have resisted injustices long before we arrived on the scene. By showing up consistently and acting collaboratively, we can develop authentic relationships of mutuality and accountability with people of colour.

...

Privilege can be a powerful tool either for being an ally or for oppression. It is important that we are mindful of how we put it to use and how we demonstrate its use in front of our children.

If we are going to change the world we live in, we will require courage, and our children will require courage. Courage to do what is right. Courage to fight for what is fair. Courage to speak up even when our voice is trembling. Courage to be uncomfortable. Courage to be unpopular. Only those who have shown courage have changed the world.

Notes

1 I acknowledge that gender is not binary and the reference to brothers and sisters in this chapter is not meant to be exclusionary of people who do not identify as either, but is merely used for ease of reference.

2 For the rest of the chapter, I have referred to these groups as people of colour for ease of reference. However, I acknowledge that some Indigenous people and black people do not identify as people of colour. The reference to people of colour in this context is not meant to trivialise or compare the experiences, current and historical, of these different groups.

3 Self determination is the right of indigenous people and black people to pursue their social, economic and cultural development and their political status. It is all about transferring decision making power to these groups of people so they can decide their own fate. Self determination also includes the reclamation of languages.

4 Microaggressions are everyday statements, actions, or incidents regarded as an instance of indirect, subtle, or unintentional discrimination against members of a marginalised group such as a racial or ethnic minority.

Reference

Guevera, C 1965, *Socialism and Man in Cuba*, 'A letter to Carlos Quijano, editor of *Marcha*', later published as *From Algiers, for Marcha: The Cuban Revolution Today*, by Che Guevara.

A colourful upbringing

Naomi Kissiedu

As I watch my children grow I start to wonder what their world has in store for them. How can we as parents help raise the next generation to effect positive change in a world that is not only changing but can also be cruel. How do I, as a parent, effectively equip them to handle these realities and to create positive change?

I will answer this question in the context of a world that is often divided by colour. A world where, for example, the colour of another person's skin is different to our own and that difference is not reflected as normal but placed into the basket of 'other.' I believe this sows a seed that separates us rather than giving rise to a mighty tree of broad branches. This is a subject I am more than familiar with as a black woman, married to a white man, and a mother of three beautiful brown-skinned children.

I am of African heritage, but British born. I married an Australian and we have three children under the age of seven. Because of my husband's work in the Australian navy, we move every two years and at the moment we live in the United States.

My children are considered Third Culture Kids (TCK). The term 'third culture kids' was first coined by researchers John and Ruth Useem in the 1950s and defines children who are raised in a culture other than their parents' nor of the culture they are legally citizens. As a result, they are often exposed to a greater variety of cultural influences because we are also a multicultural family.

Living in Australia, a country that is predominantly white, and for the most part, oblivious to its absence of true multiculturalism, I was given the opportunity to write and perform a TEDx talk. Based on my experience living in a multiracial family in various locations in Australia, I used the title 'Are you the nanny?'. This was in reference to a question asked of me numerous times by those that thought that was the most obvious answer to the skin tone difference between my children and me.

I grew up in London — one of the most ethnically diverse cities in the world. I was surrounded by different cultures and even in my own family, this was the 'norm.' After moving to Australia I realised there was a new normal! I appeared to be a minority, especially in the affluent areas, where I would constantly be asked, "where are you from?" I would reply, "London." They would then say, "no, where are you really from?" I would reply that I was born and raised in London. Then I understood. They didn't really want to know where I was born, they wanted to know about my cultural ethnicity.

What I have experienced is that in Australia my skin colour defines my ethnicity and that *British* is mostly thought of as white, any variation on that isn't understood. A person's ethnicity isn't where we are born.

We live in a very colourful country — and always have — but the truth about colour isn't being exposed. The media paint a picture of a very skewed 'normal' and my children's heroes, in their books and in the media are Caucasian families.

In this essay I'm discussing how I can equip my children with the necessary skills to create positive change during a period of global transition. At the core of this process is my fundamental belief that while our skin colour is not important, and their world view should reflect that, the history of black oppression is an important lesson to be learned and that it is important that I model courage and curiosity in the face of racism.

Race and culture through 'other' eyes

Moving to the United States of America (USA) I thought Americans would be more accepting of other cultures than Australia. I know there is a lot of history in the USA and it has its problems when it comes to racial division, but I had hoped the area we would move into would be a mixed group of different cultures and ethnicities.

Instead, we moved into a wonderful area with great schools and loads of children, but predominantly Caucasian. And once again, our dark skins weren't typical of this community. A community that, yes, is pleasant for our family, but uncomfortable around us, especially me, a black woman. We are regularly asked stereotypical questions about where we might live such as "Do you live in the flats across the way?" presumably on the assumption that we couldn't afford to live in a house.

The neighbourhood mayor invited us by email to *A Living Room Conversation* for online viewing. Thirteen people from our neighbourhood got together and talked about 'The America we want to be' and the subject was about tolerance. The mayor mentioned how the residents in the area expressed a desire to connect and converse with more Americans from diverse backgrounds.

I always hear people comment and say we need to be more tolerant of other cultures. This word 'tolerant' doesn't sit well with me because it is as if the person doesn't really want to accept someone, but is forced to do so. They ultimately believe they are superior because they don't understand people who don't share the same personal experiences and cultural background to them.

In the dictionary (lexico.com) the word 'tolerate' is defined as 'the ability or willingness to tolerate something, in particular, the existence of opinions or behaviour that one does not necessarily agree with.' So how do I address this issue with my children who are fully aware of their different skin colour, and are met with messaging that indicates they should be tolerated?

Opening things up

Multiculturalism is our global culture and so we must live this culture proactively. With increasing numbers of blended cultures living together within one family, it's important that we recognise that differences should be embraced, not tolerated, and to normalise this reality for the next generation.

Cultural mingling always happens when open up our hearts and our doors, so we can help other people be more open-minded and understanding. By doing this it will help them to be better educated. I believe people are uncomfortable with the unknown and want to put people in a box so they can feel comfortable with themselves and too often skin colour is used as the dividing line to make one group feel better than another.

We need to see people as a whole, not categorising each other, and model that behaviour with our children.

I have heard many times from parents especially from my multi-heritage social groups say that children with more than one cultural background can often feel that they must choose one culture over the other. My children of African and Caucasian descent may feel uncomfortable around Caucasian children or vice versa. We are always talking to our children about them being a beautiful mix of both our cultures, and we read books to them to help enforce that message. Although technically they are a part of both our cultures, there is still an unspoken divide that will make them feel like an outcast. We don't want them to think about picking sides, but to embrace both.

While ideas about race and multiculturalism have evolved, society still insists on classifying people in racial groups. As parents, we teach our kids about their heritage in the hope that they'll feel empowered by every part of who they are, despite confronting moments of racism due to their skin colour. Possessing some African heritage as well means that even African American history could resonate with them at some stage should they begin to self-identify more strongly with their African side.

One of the great things I have loved about moving over to the USA is the amount of African-American history and resources that are available. The information they are taught in schools about Black History they wouldn't learn anywhere else. Of course, not all of it is positive, but it is important that my children become aware of it. History and information is knowledge and they need to understand why people might behave a certain way towards us due to a long history of civil conflict.

They need to hear the difficult conversation of why our type of family was illegal many years ago, and why there are some people who still don't accept it. They need to understand that they are both black and white, while neither is important, historically this division was an extremely dark part of American history.

Confronting uncomfortable situations

Children notice more than we realise and it is imperative that they understand how the world works. Educating them on what prejudice is and how to handle a situation of discrimination will better equip them to face reality.

As parents of children who are a mix of cultures we must realise that they will face a world that may identify them as a minority. If we avoid hard and uncomfortable topics about race and pretend that people don't see colour we are teaching our children that to be 'of colour' is wrong. I have a responsibility to instil a sense of self-worth and self-confidence within my children and pretending people are colour blind will not help a child grow. In fact, it will only confuse them more when they have to confront racial discrimination.

One example of this occurred when my husband booked us to go to Virginia, to a civil war re-enactment. He felt it would be historically interesting for the family to see a re-enactment of American history.

After driving for three hours and spending the night there to arrive at the event in the morning, we stepped out of the car and when I looked around the area at the people surrounding the event, my body began to tense up. I felt a sense of discomfort: a warning is how I would describe it. I asked my husband to double check the event and find out a bit more information because I felt so uncomfortable. It wasn't because all the people were white, I've been in a room surrounded by white people most of my life, but it was because there weren't other ethnic groups. After a few minutes, my husband discovered we had come to an event that was a Confederate reenactment, and as a person of colour, I probably wouldn't have chosen to be there.

Supporters of the Confederate flag continue to claim it is a symbol of southern ancestry and heritage, as well as representing a distinct and independent cultural tradition of the Southern United States from the rest of the country. Displaying the flag has long been controversial in the United States, due to the flag's longstanding associations with racism, slavery, segregation, white supremacy, and treason (Scott Eric Kaufman, 2015: "What tradition does the Confederate flag represent?") For other supporters, the Confederate flag represents only a past era of Southern sovereignty.

The Civil War, also known as *The War Between the States* (American Battlefield Trust) was fought between the *United States of America* and the *Confederate States of America*, a collection of eleven southern states that left the Union in 1860 and 1861 to form their own country in order to protect the institution of slavery.

At that moment, I was surrounded by people who appeared to want to protect the institution of slavery. When I went up to the information stall and asked why there weren't any other people of colour, I was told that the blacks were their slaves and didn't fight. I asked, "Should I be here?" and after a very awkward pause, he answered, "You're more than welcome." But I knew I wasn't.

My son noted the tension and even asked if I should be there, and when I asked him why he thought I shouldn't be, he replied that there were no other black people. After reading more information about the re-enactment I saw that they had in fact lost the war.

My husband asked if I wanted to leave and I looked at my kids. I realised then that sometimes you need to stand strong and unapologetic of differences and embrace who we are. We needed to cherish our existence and the freedoms people of colour now rightly have. I decided to stay. My children didn't fully understand the situation we were in and wanted to play and explore, so we stayed, not for long, but enough to make our presence felt.

My daughter saw a group of women who were in charge of games and dancing. She ran over to them and asked if they could teach her their dance.

The look on these women's and men's faces indicated a discomfort. They didn't know what to do, they all looked at each other as they slowly took the hands of both my daughters and started to dance with them.

My outgoing and bubbly girls spent a good 20 minutes, chatting, dancing and playing with these women, who, in the beginning, felt confronted by our presence. By the end of our time with them, you could see they had warmed to my children. Even my son got involved in other activities that he could play on his own. I realised in that moment of discomfort for both parties that sometimes it takes a little human gesture, such as a child, to help break down barriers.

When we left I was proud that I had decided to stay. I also explained a bit about the situation to my son who was asking questions. Sometimes we are faced with discrimination and racism and we can't hide, we have to talk about it and confront it to teach our children how we can choose to behave at that moment — while assessing the level of risk or discomfort that might have surrounded us.

Travel experiences

It is important to help my children learn through the places and experiences we take them on. To help them tackle the challenges and at the same time build their confidence through experience to try new things.

We help them remember these experiences by discussing our memories. We take photos of the people and places we travel to and the friends we've made on our travels. We embrace the friendships we make along the way from people of all cultures.

Memories will be valuable in their growing life, but most importantly experiencing the positive sides of our global community is an invaluable lesson in experiencing the truth about the power of unity, over racism. Opening their eyes to new things and the wonderful experiences they can have during that exploration phase will, I hope to spark their curiosity to embrace people of all places.

I try to make sure my children see us step out of our comfort zone too. Whether they see us trying new foods, or taking on tough challenges like my TEDx Talk. I told them I was nervous doing it, but I didn't want fear to take over me. Later on, as adults, I hope they will be more empathetic and open-minded.

Technology and devices

Face-to-face communication is giving way to a new culture of online engagement like social media with applications like *Facebook*, *Instagram*, *Twitter*, and others I'm yet to discover. This faceless communication can be isolating. With so much content online there also comes our addiction to being constantly stimulated. Children no longer need people skills to engage with others because they can just use technology to stay entertained and occupied.

As parents, we often don't trust that our children are able to sit and be in their thoughts for a while or to simply play by themselves. In our household, we set ground rules that limit our children's device time until the weekend. When devices are put away my children are able to engage with other children, and adults, to have a conversation. They hear about people's stories within the context of reality, rather than in bite-sized pieces on screens.

We sit down with them over dinner and have conversations together, and we tend to utilise technology to further our conversation rather than to dominate it. My eldest will have lots of questions to ask so we sometimes ask Alexa (our virtual assistant) or we will *Google* it, or bring up clips on *YouTube* and watch the video to explore more of that certain topic. When we went to the *Black History Museum* we went home and then watched a *YouTube* documentary on all the famous black people of our time.

I mention to other parents that we don't use devices on our road trips either. My children are able to travel in the car for three to six hours and be device free because they have no other choice. Instead, they have to talk to each other, argue, play or sing to music. At home, my children rarely say "I'm bored" because they are used to playing on their own or with one another and being creative. They use their imaginations and play with what they have, and what they have is now less than they had a few months ago.

Live with less

I decided that the world's need for consuming at all times was too much, and that my children were becoming spoilt. I could see the way they treated and played with their toys as disposable objects indicated they didn't appreciate these toys or the money that they cost.

This attitude concerned me. I got my children to sort out their room and to pick out a few toys that they really enjoyed playing with. The rest I put into black bin bags and took them off to the charity bin. I have noticed with fewer toys there is less mess, which means less stress on all of us as we don't have to shout or fight about tidying up their rooms. They don't need to feel so overwhelmed by the number of toys they have to play with anymore either.

Learning and nurturing

We need to help our kids see the positive sides of diversity. We continually expose them to different food, music, books, and exhibitions, just as I do with our African (Ghanaian) culture. By travelling with us they have learned to adapt to new environments quickly, and to learn and know more than one language. My children have now started to learn Spanish at an enrichment program after school, and they are enjoying it.

Watch them grow

Every day our children are learning through us and how we interact with others. We are teaching our children how they will see the world.

My children have been lucky to experience other countries and cultures. Being exposed to different cultures from a young age will help equip our children to make a positive difference. As hard is it for my husband I have to sometimes stop him from over-parenting, from trying to protect them. My children and I have brown skin, and I know they will have to face occasional racism and discrimination. I want to emotionally prepare them for those moments, and sometimes that means letting them fail so that they can learn to build up their own self-esteem and sense of self.

As parents, we will continue to nurture their curiosity and answer their questions so they will one day go out into the world as open-minded adults empowered to stand up for positive change and manage the chaos that any major change will bring.

Notes

Naomi is the author of *The Colourful Life* book series: <https://www.bookdepository.com/Same-But-Different-Naomi-y-Kissiedu-Green/9780994465603>.

Naomi's *Tedx* talk, on the importance of teaching acceptance and diversity beyond racial and ethnic lines is available at: <https://youtu.be/Wrps-fRDqdY>.

References

Adelman, G [n.d], *The War Between the States* [Video], American Battlefield Trust, <https://www.battlefields.org/learn/videos/war-between-states>.

Kaufman, S E 2015, "What tradition does the Confederate flag represent? Is it slavery, rape, genocide, treason, or all of the above?", *salon.com*, <https://www.salon.com/2015/07/09/what_tradition_does_the_confederate_battle_flag_represent_is_it_slavery_rape_genocide_treason_or_all_of_the_above/>.

Indigenous perspectives

Happiness born of connectedness lifts up Aboriginal Australians

Larissa Behrendt

I RECENTLY SPENT some time on an outstation in the Northern Territory. Unless you have been on one, it is hard to understand the level of poverty that some Aboriginal people live in — sleeping on concrete floors, little money, no luxuries. Life is supplemented with bush tucker and everyone works together and shares what they have.

Among the basics of life, there is resilience. But there is also something else that is perhaps even more surprising. As I sat around the campfire in the evening, what rose up into the night sky amid the smoke was laughter.

This is a community surrounded by tragedy and hard social problems. This is a community with deep concerns about the impact of mining on sacred sites, about access to education, feelings of being disenfranchised and the stresses of having very little money to survive on. In nearby towns, there are issues of substance abuse and violence. So it is easy to fall into cliché and to see this laughter as being cathartic, an important release.

But there is something deeper than just the fleeting laughter that comes at the end of a funny story, a witty comment or a parody. It always strikes me in a close-knit community that something much more profound is at work. Around a campfire with shared resources — food, clothes, blankets, utensils, even shoes — there is a deep sense of contentment, a profound happiness.

Maybe the generosity of spirit creates a deeper contentment, a deeper happiness. Or maybe it is the happiness that gives a person a more generous spirit, a larger heart.

How do you take the pain of the past, whatever your background, and make it something that doesn't cripple you? How do you stop it from being a barrier to happiness?

Happiness knows no cultural barriers or bounds. But I wonder what can be learnt about true happiness from the Aboriginal women on the outstation who can illuminate the world of the rest of us.

Connected to community and country

The first lesson from my friends around the campfire is the way they look at the world around them. They see its riches.

They look at the sky and understand its meanings. They look to the land and sea around them and see additional sources of food. They look at the people who make up their family and community and they see the blessings in what they do have.

They tell stories of their fishing and hunting trips, of great romances and funny anecdotes. Their world is full of rich stories, of songlines, of music, of dance. It is impossible not to be struck by the deep interconnectedness that they have with each other and with the world around them.

When you have so very little, you are reliant on the people around you. You rely on them to share resources, to help you get from one place to another (you have to share vehicles and find a way to pay for petrol), to join together to confront a school that is not working with the community or a land council that has not been negotiating properly. And through this meaningful reliance on each other — where you don't just take but give what you have — there is deep, meaningful human connection.

This interconnectedness with other people seems to provide a strong grounding in one's own identity, one's own value, one's own place in the world. This grounding is essential for a sense of self and a sense of self-worth.

How can you be happy when you are uncomfortable with who you are? How often do we see people struggle with their identity in a way that causes them distress and misery? There is none of that among people who are deeply rooted in their community and have a strong sense of their place.

There is also interconnectedness to the natural world. The women on the outstation have been hunting turtles and fishing in the waters since they were small girls. They know which plants are edible and they know what fruit is edible.

They also know the stories about the creation of the world around them, how the constellations in the sky were formed and the songlines about great trips across the country. In the world around them, there are stories and legends but there is also knowledge of the seasons and an ability to read the landscape and the weather.

Research shows that people who live on the outstations have better health than those living in town. These are alcohol-free communities but their diets are also better as a result of the richness of the food found in the land and sea, which supplements the processed, unhealthy food.

In these remote areas, fresh food is expensive. Lollies, soft drink and processed foods are cheap. Diets are poor and health is poor as a result. So on the outstations, where fruits, vegetables, fish, turtles and other bush food supplement diets, it is easy to see why people are healthier.

Lives enriched by creativity

So it is easy to see how the interconnectedness to country is also a source of a contented life. But there is something else that engages the women here, something that is linked to their culture but also seems to be a basic element in fundamental happiness. They have a very rich creative life.

The women of this community — and some of the men — are gifted painters. They translate the stories told by their parents and grandparents into vivid canvasses. They express themselves as eloquently through their brush strokes as they do with their words.

In addition to their painting, they have their traditional songs, their songlines and their dance. They are creative performers of their cultural traditions and they not only perform but teach the children the same songs and dances.

And between the painting, the dancing and the music is a rich traditional of storytelling as old as the culture. These women are natural storytellers. Although they have not written the stories, they perform them in the way they tell them. They are the expression of the vibrancy of the world's oldest living culture.

Living in close proximity to others is not easy and this is a community where there is overcrowding. On fine nights, people sleep under the stars, but there are not enough rooms for the number of people here and so people share concrete floors when they have to.

So life is not without its arguments and disagreements, its jealousies and bickering and all of the other things that happen between people who live closely. But the generosity and openness of the women who have the moral leadership in this community is defined by the love they have for their families, especially their children.

There is no romance in being poor, but there is happiness to be found when you can find the richness in life. That is the abiding lesson I learn from my visits to this other way of life.

And as the laughter rings around the campfire, and I listen to the women, all sisters, sing their songs, teach the children to dance, tell their ancient stories, gently tease each other — and me — it is a reminder that there are ties that are deeper than blood and that lightness of spirit is the measure of happiness.

This essay first appeared in The Conversation *(theconversation.com/au) and is reproduced here with kind permission of the author.*

Feelings can be wrong

Nelly Thomas

So why can't we be still, why can't we love each other?
Is kindness an ancient skill buried by our blindness?
And if we look behind us there's a wind blowing in
To create the age of reason

Age of Reason, John Farnham, 1988
Written by Todd Hunter and Johanna Pigott.

ONE CAN NEVER REALLY tell if they're raising the next generation well. Surely our parents — and theirs before them — thought they were doing a terrific job while in truth, like all of us, they were doing their best and that best sometimes came up short. The most we can hope for is that we go into the future thoughtfully and with kindness.

And like every generation that ever was, for this guidance, I return to the music of my youth: the 1980s and John Farnham. *Age of Reason* and *You're the Voice* were the soundtracks of my youth. I was born and raised in 1970/80's rural Western Australia and despite the stereotypes, I was surrounded by culture (including Farnsey). It just wasn't one respected by the elite. There were good and bad reasons for this.

On the plus side, we had wonderful music. And by wonderful, I mean mainstream working-class rock and pop. I still place *Working Class Man* in the category of poetry and have never been more stirred by a piece of art than by Barnesy's *Flame Trees*.

We also enjoyed a fabulous array of television, from *Prisoner* to *The Price is Right*, and from *A Country Practice* to *Sale of the Century*. In the circles I now move in, when I mention these shows, people think I am mocking them or being ironic; but I am not. *Prisoner* was a revolutionary show with an almost all-female cast, none of whom looked like Barbie. *The Price is Right* had contestants that looked and sounded like my aunties, uncles and parents. *A Country Practice* was set in a rural location, but offered a much more kind and inclusive vision of country life to the one I experienced. And *Sale of the Century* showed me that being smart was okay; that the pursuit of knowledge was worthy.

I was not exposed to theatre, opera, literature, art or overseas travel in my youth. The first live performance I saw was when Albie Mangles visited town on one of his world tours, and I didn't see a ballet until I was 44-years-old. But I had ideas, art, and philosophies on life — *culture* — all around me.

On the negative side, my town was extraordinarily harsh to outsiders. While we had a significant Indigenous population, the racism was palpable, clear and overt. Friendships with Indigenous kids were tolerated up until early primary school and longer if, and only if, the black kid was good at sport. By the age of about ten we feared *them* and I can only assume they feared *us*. A lasting memory of my childhood is hearing adults (whom I loved and adored) discuss an older Aboriginal woman in town who would deliberately get arrested so she could get a meal and safe bed for the night in the lock-up. They mocked her, they referred to her in racist language, and they spoke of her with utter contempt. To this day, I don't understand how anyone could see this woman's desperation as a funny anecdote.

I recount this memory, not to shame my town or the people in it, but because it was — and in some parts, still is — the truth. While our town embodied all the country charm, the camaraderie and the sense of community that rural Australia represents in the public imaginary, it was also a very hostile place for those who didn't fit in. In some ways, it is a microcosm of wider Australia.

...

I am now a writer and a comedian and appear regularly on the telly and radio. I live in the northern suburbs of Melbourne. For those unfamiliar with the area, while I am not in the inner city, I live in literally the most progressive electorate in the nation. There is a mix of rich and poor, many cultures, ethnicities and religions, a range of sexualities, lifestyles and general vibes. In relative terms it's a welcoming and inclusive place.

In my street, for example, we have a mix of same-sex families, non-English-speaking neighbours, people in public housing, white-collar professionals and artists. African teenagers from a group-home walk past almost every day, there are sketchy guys in hoodies with tell-tale drawn faces, and nosey nonnas literally knock on my door and tell me I'm gardening wrong. There are three Muslim families (that I know of) and one of them is from a refugee background. Our kids all go to school together and the Muslim refugee bloke is our electrician. We're not in each other's faces, but if I hear the fire alarm going off in one of their homes I go over and check that everything is okay. At Christmastime, Anna (a devout Portuguese Christian) from over the road comes bearing gifts for the kids. (Side note: when Anna's dog misbehaves, she tells it off for *insulting Jesus*).

While I desperately miss the stillness of country life, the expansive warm wheat fields of my youth and the drop-in cups of tea, the street I now live in is the vision of Australia I prefer — a big fat melting pot of people, which occasionally boils over and causes a bit of a mess. If you could take my street and plop it somewhere warm and lush like North Queensland, I'd move there in an instant.

I am always in-between, never quite at home.

In a sense, this is a good thing. I stand betwixt old and new Australia. I was raised on John Williamson, Princess Di and Rodney Rude (who, incidentally still tours) but I have created a life that is more in line with The Hilltop Hoods,

Fear of a Brown Planet and AFLW. I am a True Blue Aussie, but I will not be limited by the idea. I am a patriot who is supremely grateful to live in Australia, but I recognise Nation States as made-up things.

I also seek to know and learn more of Australia pre-colonisation; when the land I stand upon was considered by all to be sacred. I claim neither religion, nor spirituality, but I am not stupid enough to think *the oldest living culture on earth* has nothing to teach me. In my area, the Kulin nation tribes believe the earth was created by Bunjil, the mighty Eagle, who asked only two things of visitors: to not harm the children or land of Bunjil. Don't get me wrong, I am an atheist and I don't *literally* believe that an Eagle created the earth, but if I were going to accept a non-scientific theory of creation I would most certainly choose one that simply said *look after the earth and her children* over one that said you'll go to hell for being gay or, everything will be alright once you're dead if you just do what I say.

...

What does all this have to do with raising the next generation of humans to be *kind*? The way I see it, we are at a crossroads in both Australia and the world. The old ways — institutionalised religion, patriarchy, monarchy are gone:

> *Now that our fathers have gone*
> *[We've] been left to carry on*
>
> Age of Reason, John Farnham, 1988
> Written by Todd Hunter and Johanna Pigott.

But we haven't yet replaced them with another belief system. Or we have — neo-liberal extreme capitalism is rampant — yet we *know* this serves neither humans nor the planet.

> *What about the world around us*
> *How can we fail to see?*
> *What about the age of reason*
>
> Age of Reason, John Farnham, 1988
> Written by Todd Hunter and Johanna Pigott.

So, what to do? In moving forward, is the choice either reason or emotion? If so, what do both of these mean?

I see reason, in the sense of the Enlightenment, as the absence of irrational nonsense. Forgive me for characterising religion and spirituality as such, but even the most devout follower of any religion cannot deny the atrocities that have been done, and are still being done, in the name of religion and of God but which are in reality just the cruel, selfish and reckless brandishing of human power. One need look no further than the catastrophic abuse of children by churches of nearly all denominations (and arguably worse, the *acceptance* and cover-up of this abuse) to demonstrate the corrupting nature of irrational and unearned power.

And let's not forget that witches were burned at the stake, or that in some countries women are still stoned to death for being *raped*, or that many Americans voted for a man who admitted to grabbing women by the genitals without their consent and who claims to be Christian. Our own current Prime Minister offers pictures of himself in Church praying while overseeing an immigration regime that denies a two-year old child a birthday cake (Davidson, 2019). There is nothing vaguely *reasonable* about any of this and yet, it is the *do-gooders* like me who are routinely accused of being *too emotional*.

On the other hand, I worry about the ascendancy of *feelings* as the basis off both our beliefs and actions; hence the title of this essay: feelings can be wrong. I am desperate to see more compassion, kindness and love — more feeling — in our leaders and yet, I am terrified of the ubiquitous phrase *that's just how I feel*.

Feelings can be wrong.

I may well *feel* scared of a black man walking behind me on the street, but that feeling is not right; it is called racism. The *feeling* of fear is real, but the reality of the danger is not; I am far more at risk from the men I know and love. If I am ever killed by a man (sorry for the horror thought), the police will question my partner first, then ex-boyfriends, then men I am friends with, then uncles and so on. They do this for a reason.

Racism is an ideology that leads to *feelings* that can be wrong.

Same goes for sexism, homophobia, ableism and all the other systems of belief that indoctrinate us to feel uneasy around people we see as different from ourselves.

Those feelings are wrong.

The other problem with unchecked feelings is that they can lead just as quickly to nastiness, as they can to kindness. This might be as benign as just taking an instant dislike to someone for no real reason, or as harmful as *feeling* that Aboriginal kids would just be better off with white families. (Note here that I have no doubt that many of the people in the organisations responsible for the Stolen Generation *felt* they were doing the right thing.)

In the modern context, just take a quick squiz at social media to see how toxic *feelings* can be. I think there are many wonderful things about social media but it is also Exhibit A of a what a world with unchecked feelings looks like. I *feel* angry, therefore I will direct that anger at you. I *feel* sad, therefore you *made* me sad. I *feel* inadequate and so I will do whatever I can to bring you down to my level. *I have a shit-tonne of feelings I can't handle and I will spray them randomly at whomever I can, regardless of consequence for them or me.*

Feelings are also the seemingly impenetrable barrier that exists between my old life and my new, between John Williamson and Moana Hope, between Old Australia and New Australia (which is really the Idea of Australia and the Reality of Australia).

We can't talk to each other because of our *damn feelings.*

Old Australia is *feeling* scared of immigrants, queers, technology, foreigners and mouthy broads. New Australia is *feeling* furious at old white guys, Christians, rich people and Queenslanders. We're all yelling at each other, we're all making assumptions and almost none of us are listening or being kind.

Meanwhile, we're all telling our kids to play nice. Much like we tell them not to lie and then in the same breath say it's rude when they say they find it boring it at Grandma's. But I digress.

Let me be clear that I am not saying there is a general equivalence between the fear an old white guy has of 'Muslims being Terrorists' and the fear that a Muslim woman walking into a country pub has. In the latter case, the fear is well founded and for her to *not* live with some element of fear would frankly, be dangerous. In the former, he's watching too much *A Current Affair*. But what I am saying, is that those of us with the voice and opportunity to use that voice serve absolutely no good purpose by just yelling at that old white guy and calling him names.

Let's take Trump. I do not especially want to write about Donald Trump in an anthology on kindness but we cannot ignore him and what he represents if we want a better, kinder future for our kids. Trump was elected for a range of reasons. One was racism. No doubt he played on the racism endemic in America toward African-Americans (including Barak Obama), Muslims and immigrants in particular.

Let me go on a brief tangent here and tell you about an experience I had with our neighbours. About 12 years ago we moved to our current home and as I have already indicated, it's a multicultural melting pot. Our neighbours are elderly, first generation Italian migrants, speak little English and literally have a market garden in their back yard. They bring homemade wine over and despite 12 years of conversations over the fence, they get both of our names wrong. They are kind and generous. But the day we moved in, one of the first things they said to us was: "We are so glad you moved here, good Australian family, and not the Chinese." These are people who would have once been called 'wogs' and 'dagos,' and told to go back where they came from. They were the Chinese of the 1980s and 1990s, the Muslims of the 2000s and the Africans of today. It makes no sense.

But it sort of does.

In short, I suspect that they were *feeling relieved* to not be the ones in the firing line. When a new target comes into town, they move up a notch in the pecking order and can either stay in the trenches and fight, or wield their new privilege. I suspect this also happened — and is still happening — in America. The white working poor once had the *feeling* of at least being *superior* in racial terms. They were poor but they were white and their race was dominant. Then Oprah came along and redefined television, Jay-Z bought a basketball team and Barak Obama got elected. They *felt* like they lost their position on the ladder, their white privilege, and as we can know from other movements, equality can *feel* like oppression when you're used to unearned privilege. (And you can feel oppressed even when all the evidence suggests you're still well ahead.)

So, racism existed, Trump tapped into it and to this day he continues to stoke it for his own ends: power. I honestly don't know if he even believes the racist things he says and does. His only concerns are power and money and he will do whatever it takes to get and hold onto both.

The other reason Trump was elected was that the elite *have* ignored white working-class America for decades. In fact, the only time they seem to take any notice of them at all is when they're the butt of a joke: trailer trash, rednecks, real housewives of somewhere (new money, but still…) or when they need bodies for a war.

> This town is not the kind of place
> That moneyed people go
> They make their jokes up on the TV
> About all the snow
> And they're building condos downriver
> From where the plant had been
> But nobody really lives here
> Now that the air is clean

Trickle Down, Ani DiFranco, 1999

The working classes are not stupid. They know the gap between rich and poor is growing, they know their jobs are going and they only have to look down the street to see and *feel* that there *are* other people doing better.

Imagine living in a country that has the best medical services in the world and then watching your dad die of cancer because he can't afford health insurance. Imagine seeing home renovation shows where people throw out all their furniture and buy new stuff when you can't afford to turn the heater on. Imagine working for five generations in a timber mill, only to see 20-year-old green activists screaming at you: *No Jobs on a Dead Planet*. Optimism requires a sense of future. This is a *feeling* the working poor haven't had in America for a long time. And they are not wrong: the rich are getting richer, and they *are* being left behind.

Then imagine a guy you've seen on the TV, who talks 'truth' to power and sounds a *little bit more like you*, who comes along and says: "I'm going to make America Great Again!"

I know you're scared, am I'm going to tell you why! You can't afford the doctor, or university or even to pay your rent and it's because THE MEXICANS ARE COMING.

You are scared to go to the movies in case you get shot, and it's because THE MUSLIMS ARE COMING.

You aren't even allowed to hit your kids anymore and it's because THE WOMEN DON'T KNOW THEIR PLACE.

THE QUEERS WANT GENDER-NEUTRAL BATHROOMS.

THE FEMINISTS WANT ABORTION.

THE GREENIES WANT TO TAKE AWAY YOUR JOBS.

When the fear-centre of the brain is activated, all reason is lost. It doesn't matter that the real reason the gap between rich and poor is growing is capitalist greed, or that you'll more likely get shot by a white supremacist, or that hitting kids doesn't work, or that you have a gender-neutral bathroom in your own house, or that abortion isn't mandatory or that the future of jobs is in green energy. You are literally not thinking straight; you are flooded with *emotion*. And it turns out the amygdala will override even the most rational animal.

So, you've got this TV guy (celebrity as a concept is also irrational, but very powerful) presidential candidate who says he sees you, says he knows you and even better, he says he can make it all better. The joke is on them now, not you! Then you've got the baseline historical racism, sexism and homophobia on which the nation was founded. It is lurking, waiting to burn the next witch. It has taught you that you are owed more than *them*. Then you've got the reality right in front of your face of either insecure or no work at all, of medicine you can't afford and schools you can't get into. And THEN you have a TV and social media stream giving you 24-hour-news, with more information and tragedy than the human brain was ever supposed to cope with.

And so you have a perfect storm of irrationality: I *feel* out of control, so I will elect someone who will *assert control*. A patriarch who will literally burn the world to the ground to get his way. Finally, daddy is back in charge.

Imagine instead, if the elite, even the bleeding heart do-gooders like me, had listened to some of these people instead of talking at them *before Trump came along*. Imagine if we'd heard their fear, instead of mocked their spelling or the fact that they'd never been on a plane. Imagine if those of us with power — economic, cultural, social, political — had used it to bring them inside the tent, instead of laughing at their faces pressed up against the glass.

Would it have prevented Trump? I honestly don't know, but moving forward, I think two ears, one mouth is all we've got.

. . .

So, what does all this mean for parenting; for raising future humans who are kind?

First and foremost it means establishing a connection between our kids and other humans. We are nothing without other people and while kids don't have to be *popular*, they must have a connection to community — to both give and receive love, kindness and help.

Also, their own personal feelings must be are honoured, but within limits and tempered by thought. My kids, for example, are not asked to hug people they don't want to (this sends the wrong message about consent), but we do insist that they say hello to everyone coming to our home. We do not expect them to like everyone, but they must have a reason to dislike someone. And if that reason is irrational or prejudiced because, for example, they're a different religion or talk funny, we will strongly challenge it.

Our kids are strictly expected to have manners. Whether someone is a complete stranger or their best friend, they must say please, thank you, hello, goodbye and all the other stuff. They must offer hospitality and be generous. Of course, there is a limit to this. If someone comes into our home and is rude, cruel or recklessly offensive *and will not change*, I will challenge them, and even ask them to leave if I have to. We're not in the habit of jumping down people's throats though. I know that many of the people I grew up with would, for example, use racist language but once challenged would be mortified to know they'd caused offence and stop it. (I also know many people who would never use racist language but are arseholes.) In short, I am not saying you never throw an elbow, but I am saying it is the last resort.

On a related note, I have noticed in my public life, that *feelings* can be a very valuable tool to neutralise intolerance and even cruelty. People on the radio and TV are meant to pretend to not have feelings (which is part of the reason they/we are both reified and vilified) but I have found being open and honest about feelings has lead to some profound exchanges with fans and foes alike. The most obvious of these is personal attacks I've received either live on stage or on social media and in the comments sections of radio, TV and other media work. I don't generally read the comments sections, but if people contact me and are rudely critical or often, just downright mean, I will either ignore, ask them questions or, sometimes I'll tell them they've *hurt my feelings*. The same can be done with friends, family members and colleagues who say offensive things: *you hurt my feelings*.

It is surprisingly effective in many instances. And it's so simple.

Oftentimes, the person being rude is *angry* (usually nothing at all to do with you or what you've said) and when you name your own feelings, they are forced to confront theirs:

> *You hurt my feelings.*
> *What am I feeling?*
> *I am angry.*

I don't for a second mean to suggest that all bigots are to be pitied, tolerated or engaged with, but I do think that until someone is *obviously* and *deliberately* being cruel or bigoted, then engage with them if *you have the time and energy.* How else will we ever be able to talk to each other and face the profound challenges coming at us as a species?

The last bit requires a bit more attention: *if you have the time and energy*.

The other thing I am teaching my kids is that they do not owe themselves to everyone, and certainly not all the time. Both are girls and it is especially important that they know that it is not their job to fix everyone; to fix men in particular. Service to others is critical to an ethical life, but slavery to others — even having to always be nice regardless of how others treat you — is a form of self-harm. It is not only okay, but also essential, to look after you and yours and to have good boundaries. Martyrs are not good role models; spoiler alert: Joan of Arc dies in the end.

Of course, all this thinking about power and how to wield it, needs to be balanced with a sobering and contemplative understanding of where you sit in the world and what privilege you have. Many of my family members used to play 'a game' with me whereby they'd throw out deliberately provocative statements at family gatherings to bait me. They seemed to find winding me up amusing, even when it was obviously causing me pain. That's wrong and there's no excuse for it. On the other hand, with age, I can now see that I was also reckless. I was the first in my family to be afforded the opportunity to go to university. I had educational, and therefore life, opportunities that they never had. I was often aggressive with my use of language and I wielded the power of my intellect and education without kindness.

I now believe that you cannot be progressive if you are *unkind*.

If you have a voice and you don't make space for the voices of others, if you don't lift others up with you, I don't care how clever or right you are, you are doing more harm than good. I want my kids to know that the very best thing they can be is not rich, famous or influential but *kind*, to themselves and to others. Ironically, this may just be the way to create the age of reason.

Being an intensely practical person, I will sum up with some practical tips:

One: we should teach our kids to judge people not what they *say*, but on what they *do*. We only need to look at The Donald to see that people can *say anything*; what they *do* matters most. This, ironically, also applies to 'the opposition.' While language is extraordinarily powerful, there is far too much writing people off for simply getting terminology wrong. As someone with an autistic child, I can tell you that it hurts when people use terms like 'disordered' to describe her magnificent brain, but I also understand that this is no reason to dismiss them out of hand. Some of the kindest, most inclusive and emotionally intelligent people in our wider circle get these terms wrong but *do the right thing*. Conversely, some of the people who know all the right things to say, make little to no effort with her at all. This lesson also applies to romantic relationships, family and friendships. Anyone can say *I love you*, but what do they *do*?

Two: teach your kids — and yourself — to look at your tent, to closely examine their own social, school and work circles. Who is in them and why? More importantly, who is *not* in them and why.

You cannot make the world a better place without using whatever power and influence you have to bring others in and hopefully, up with you. You cannot do this alone or, with other people exactly like you. This is hard and will sometimes come at a cost to you. I had a recent situation where an organisation that wanted to work with me would not make some pretty easy adaptations to make their events more disability accessible. I politely called them on it and the result was that I lost work. I also lost the collegiate friendships I had formed there and, to some extent, some influence. This is not something I did lightly or without some regret, but at the end of the day, words of inclusion may be nice but if people are excluded from participating because they literally can't get in the building, those words don't mean a lot. The older I get and more established my career is, the more opportunities I have to make a fuss when a fuss needs to be made.

Finally: raising good kids is all about equality.

Equality is a moral aim in and of itself, but it's also practical. If history teaches us anything it's that the downtrodden, *the masses*, will rise up eventually. In a very bizarre way, this is modern America — the progressive elite *did* ignore the widening gap between rich and poor, and while they were busy amassing wealth and power, a kind of revolution began. The rest of us can learn from this.

Wealth and comfort are relative concepts. In Australia, almost all of us are relatively well off compared to the rest of the world. But humans don't compare ourselves to the 'rest of the world,' we compare our living standards to those in our community, our country; to those we can see. Unlike some, you may have a home, but if you can't afford to fix your gutters and meanwhile your landlord is on their third investment property, they will be unrecognisable to you. If one of us is struggling to feed the family while the other is redecorating seasonally, how can we come together as a community? If a child took seven pieces of cake at their birthday party and left all the guests with one piece to share, we'd blast them. We need to share the cake.

. . .

In short, I am flying blind with raising kids as much as many of you are and, maybe, as much as generations past. I don't know if I'll be successful. The only thing I know is to teach them, and to model to them, the extraordinary power of kindness and generosity. I had surgery a few years ago after losing a baby. It was devastating. I do not remember the name of the surgeon, the anaesthetist, or the CEO of the hospital but I do remember the face of the nurse who held my hand and smiled at me when I woke up. I felt seen and held. When all hope feels lost, I remember that feeling and how it changed me. That is power.

> *This time, we know we call can stand together*
> *With the power to be powerful*
> *Believing, we can make it better*
>
> You're The Voice, John Farnham, 1991
> Written by Andy Qunta, Keith Reid,
> Maggie Ryder, and Chris Thompson

Reference

Davidson, H 2019, 'Detention centre denies two-year-old Tamil girl a birthday cake,' *The Guardian*, <https://www.theguardian.com/australia-news/2019/jun/18/detention-centre-denies-two-year-old-tamil-girl-a-birthday-cake>.

Safe enough to innovate
Protecting our kids' creative futures

Anna Lidstone

"What if there's snakes?"
"What if we get lost?"
"What if it rains?"

I'm in the middle of a forest with a group of eight-year-olds, surrounded by that buzz of nervous energy that kids emit when they're out of school on an excursion.

"What if…" is known as a catalytic question in creativity. If we use it properly, it can catalyse potential, open up possibility and expand the horizons of the future. And then sometimes, like now, it just opens up a torrent of anxiety and fear.

As we stand in a clearing, the teacher gives the kids their first challenge: to find five new things around them that they have never seen before.

"That's not fair," one kid protests. "I come here all the time. There's nothing I haven't seen before."

"Well, I've never been in a forest," says another. "So it's going to be easy for me to find new things."

"What if we can't find anything?" one demands to know, obviously a fan of clear consequences.

"I've been to a forest four times," another says to the first. "So I've seen a lot of it too, but maybe not as much as you."

A chorus of high-pitched childish voices chime in, all offering up their own forest experiences and predicting how much newness they would find. They unanimously agree that that the kids with the most forest experience are at a disadvantage, while those who have never spent time in forests will find the challenge easy. My ears prick up at the makings of this informal study.

And then they set off to look for their new things.

The kids' predictions are logical and reasonable. They sound accurate. But … they are completely wrong.

The kids who say they had no experience in the forest struggle to find even a couple of things they haven't seen before. For them, it seems, a leaf is a leaf. Of course they've seen a tree before, so they can't include that. Several say that the forest feels "scary" and are visibly uncomfortable. Some struggle with the fact that there don't seem to be any 'right' answers, and need reassurance from adults that they are doing okay. They work alone, and soon complain that the activity is "boring" and "dumb."

The kids who say they are very familiar with the forest, though, find five things quickly, then 10 or 20, and then stop counting because they are too absorbed in how many interesting and new things they can find. Excited and energised, they work together unselfconsciously, eager to share their enthusiasm and build on each other's ideas. They find hundreds of new things: a different shade of green, an unfamiliar insect, a strange texture on a high branch, a bigger or smaller rock, the tiny dots on a familiar purple flower, a leaf with an unusually shaped hole, an unfamiliar kind of nest, an unusual ridge in a termite's mound...

In other words, these kids — from the same school, with similar backgrounds — have vastly different reactions to the task. Those who are comfortable, familiar and feel safe in the forest have a much higher capacity for seeing, and creating, 'newness' than those who feel unsafe.

COMFORTABLE. FAMILIAR. SAFE. These are all dirty words in creativity and innovation. We're supposed to be uncomfortable, and unsafe, and embrace situations that are scary and unfamiliar. We're supposed to have to stretch and rely on our resilience to handle the unknown.

We share cute little diagrams like this with each other, and everyone says

"Ooh. Profound," and pledges to step outside their comfort zone and take more personal and creative risks.

But this isn't the full story.

As well as a parent and writer, I am also a creativity and innovation consultant. I work with organisations and individuals to help them solve complex problems and teach them how to be more innovative. So I know a few things about the art and science of creative thinking.

And what happened in the forest doesn't surprise me one bit (although I was delighted that the 'study' played out so unambiguously).

Because the worst kept secret among anyone who works in the field of creativity is this:

There is no creativity without safety

Kids who play *Minecraft* know that there are two settings. There's creative mode, where you can build something new, and there's survival mode, where you, well, survive. And kids understand that when you're in survival mode, you can't be in creative mode. The adults in their life, though, are slower on the uptake. This essay isn't about *Minecraft* but it is about 'creative mode.'

It's become a bit of a cliché that the world is full of complex problems that the next generation is responsible for solving. "No pressure," we tell our young teenagers, "but your generation is going to be single-handedly responsible for solving a whole bunch of big hairy problems." And we rattle them off: climate change, population explosion, refugee-ism, food and resource security, antibiotic resistance, the rise of fundamentalism, disease epidemics, the new robotic world order and a hundred — a thousand — more. "So you're going to have to be innovative to solve all these problems," we tell them.

But at the same time, we seem hell bent on doing everything we can to prevent our kids from having access to 'creative mode.'

"Now wait a minute," I hear you protest. "How can you claim that? We're always talking about supporting our kids' innovation. What about those government ads about the innovation economy? What about all the new tech start-ups? Didn't the school just hold (another) fundraiser for their state-of-the-art 'innovation lab'? All our kids do group work every single day so they learn how to collaborate. 18-year-olds can become CEOs of well-endowed companies, just by designing a cool new app. Everyone's talking about 'design thinking.' Even our three-year-olds can use a electronic tablet. Anna, how can you possible accuse us of holding our kids back from their creative potential as the problem-solvers of the future?"

Well, I'll tell you. We're not keeping our kids safe enough to innovate.

We think we're keeping them safe. That is, after all, one of our main jobs as parents. We plug them into car seats, and use tiny screws to keep toy batteries out of their mouths, and keep our poisons on the top shelf. We choose our schools carefully, looking for pastoral care programs and a commitment to anti-bullying programs. And we drive them to school and put them into organised programs with blue card holders, and we tuck them in at night and lock the doors.

But we're not keeping them 'psychologically safe.' Not psychologically safe enough to innovate, anyway.

This secret – that there is no creativity without safety — is such a badly kept one that *Google* released a major study in 2014 confirming it. They analysed all of their teams to try to work out what factors had the biggest influence on the success of a team. Academic background? Leadership style? Age of the team members? Access to sleeping pods and ping pong tables? And they found that, consistently, their highest-performing teams were those which scored high on psychological safety — the feeling that the conditions were in place for people to be able to take creative risks, without fear of reprisal or judgement from their team.

And yet in Australia, as in many Western countries, we have been moving further away from the conditions that would make kids feel comfortable with innovation, even as we crack the metaphorical whip at them and tell them to "Innovate, innovate, innovate." When a major study was conducted in Australia on psychological safety, young workers experienced the least amount of psychological safety of them all.

To explain what I mean, I'd like to introduce you to Jamie, an imaginary friend of mine who is growing up right now, in middle-class Australia.

Jamie's parents care about her deeply and want the best for her future, so, at the age of three, they put her into an academically-inclined preschool, which promises to prepare her for a rapidly changing, technologically-rich twenty-first century.

It's different from what they remember as kids. Nowhere near as much play and a lot more use of digital whiteboards. They are both relieved about this, as they both used to play a lot, often for hours at a time outside with the local kids, and they want Jamie to have a better life than they did. Jamie learns to read by the time she starts school.

When Jamie goes to school, they choose a local private school full of families 'just like them.' They want Jamie to fit in and have friends. They are happy to see that the school has very high academic standards — they can tell because of the high scores on standardised tests published on the website. They are also pleased that it has a 'rigorous curriculum' where nothing is left to chance. The kids are given clear learning 'outcomes' that are rigorously tested and measured. They like the fact that the curriculum is standardised, so they know that Jamie isn't missing out on anything compared to other kids in Australia. The kids learn to code and there is a strong emphasis on STEM, which is a phrase that's new to them but which they learnt means science, technology, engineering and maths. These are the skills of the future, and they want her to be prepared. She has a lot of homework each night, to help her develop good study skills, so she can get into a good high school and be assured a fantastic future. They make sure she doesn't fall between the cracks.

Like all kids, Jamie is sometimes messy and leaves craft projects around the house. But they proudly nip that in the bud early on and teach her to keep the house tidy. She can always do messy art projects at school, during that last week of term when all the important content is finished.

They drive her to school every day, as they know that it's not safe for her to walk. On the weekends, to relax, they take her to the park. All kids need some downtime sometimes. They scorn the parents who sit on the bench at the side, uninvolved in their kids' lives, choosing instead to be actively engaged in Jamie's play time. Ever the good parents, they remind her not to go too high on the climbing frame, and call out "be careful" and "watch out" at regular intervals because they don't want her to fall and hurt herself.

At high school, they encourage Jamie to do well. It's a competitive high school, with more high standards. Places are scarce but Jamie has had private tutoring and won herself a spot. It's important that she does well. The future is uncertain, university places are hard to get and jobs are highly competitive. She studies hard and is often one of the first to know the answers. She has never failed at school, not even a single test or piece of assessment, something of which she is very proud. The school makes sure that their expectations are clear and that the students know what success looks like.

After school, she does activities or homework club. They don't want her to have too much time on her hands, and it's important to 'keep her busy' to keep her out of trouble. It's so hard to keep teenage girls safe.

In her junior years, she tries out some art subjects. She's a good student and adeptly works out what the teacher wants to see so she can keep up her grades. In senior years, she thinks about doing art history, but it's a hard subject and she's not really sure how to get an A in it. It all seems very subjective and airy-fairy. And it's time to get serious now anyway so, with her parents' encouragement, she chooses business and accounting subjects instead. She sees a counsellor briefly when she gets a bit sad in high school, to help her to build her 'resilience.'

There's no question of her doing any arts or humanities subjects in university. She's a good student from a good family. Her grades are strong and she has oodles of potential. Why would she throw all that away? She wants to get a 'good job.' She is delighted when she gets accepted into a business/economics program at the local university. Her future is bright.

At this point, she is old enough to float onto my radar, since I typically work with adults. Let's just say, for this thought experiment, that she finds herself in one of my programs to solve some big hairy problem.[1]

And in this context, I will introduce her to some of the foundational principles and values that underpin my work in creativity and innovation. (It's my job to take these principles and turn them into actions and behaviours.) These include:

- Finding the sweet spot of 'flow' and 'optimal anxiety'
- Tolerance for ambiguity and complexity
- Imagination
- Risk taking
- A sense of belonging, supported by inclusivity and diversity
- Emotional intelligence (including compassion, empathy, morality, ethics)
- A commitment to the shared vision of the group

Ah. As some obscure writer called Shakespeare said: *Therein lies the rub.*

You see, these values aren't really the same ones that Jamie brings into the workshop. And, nothing against Jamie — she's a lovely young adult and is keen to work hard to impress me — but we may have a bit of a problem.

Let me explain.

Firstly, Jamie is likely to have spent large amounts of her life in survival mode, not creative mode. Around 70 percent of teenagers in Australia report high levels of stress. Around half of them will have suffered from diagnosable depression and anxiety.

This is a problem, not just because we want our kids to be happy, but also because stress hijacks our neurological pathways. The 'reptilian' part of our brain gets activated by stress, which essentially puts the brain into survival mode, and, like *Minecraft* says, you can either be in survival mode or creative mode and not both. Stress in the short term might spark creativity — which is why deadlines can be very motivating — but over the long term undermines our ability to think creatively.

High levels of competition, high stakes demands and a scarcity mentality (where we feel that we have to compete for basic resources) all make this stress worse. Jamie has experienced all of these for most of her life.[2] This will be compounded because her stress, depression or anxiety haven't been offset by extensive free play or time spent pursuing the arts, both of which have been shown to reduce stress in both children and adults.

In the workshop, I will be working hard to stay with the 'optimal anxiety' zone — which is just enough stress to be motivating and not enough to send the brain into survival mode. I will also be introducing the idea of 'flow' — that wonderful feeling where you're so absorbed that you lose track of time, which is also affected by too much anxiety (as well as too much boredom). But this group, neurologically, may find it difficult to stay out of the anxiety zone.

If I had in my group a cross-section of the population as a whole,[3] in addition to young adults like Jamie, I would also have young adults who had been raised in poverty — 17 percent of kids in Australia in fact. Poverty has also been shown to have an effect on the neurology of creativity, sending the brain into survival mode.

So that will be my group.

The first thing I establish when I'm working with a new client is whether the problem they are trying to solve is a good fit for creative problem solving. We are looking for problems that are complex, ambiguous, and have multiple possible answers. There can't be a single answer or solution, or an off-the-shelf solution, or even an answer that just requires a bit of research. There will be times when participants won't even be sure what the question is, let alone what the possible answers might be. Even those who have a high tolerance for ambiguity will find themselves tested.

And yet, the vast majority of the young adults in this hypothetical group will have had relatively low exposure to ambiguity and complexity. They will have been raised in a system where curricular is standardised, and where, as a result, outcomes need to be predictable and measurable. They will have been trained in coming up with single, correct answers, often measured on a multiple choice test. Their ability to do this will have determined, to a large extent, their 'success' in the system.

Even 'longer answers' formats, such as NAPLAN writing tests, will have taught them to produce formulaic, simplistic responses, usually without the chance to do multiple drafts, research, edit, or develop nuanced arguments. They will have probably have a STEM background, which may or may not have helped them to develop complex critical thinking skills, but often minimal training in the arts and humanities.[4]

In their spare time, they will have 'consumed' social media soundbites, where complex ideas are reduced to a few hundred characters, opinions are reduced to simple binaries, and academic research is summarised into short pithy articles for popular consumption.[5]

I once watched my Mum jump out of an aeroplane, as part of a tandem parachute jump. Her face was pure terror. But it would be nothing compared to the terror that would probably be on Jamie's face if she was suddenly thrown into a highly ambiguous situation without support or scaffolding.

To get people to think beyond the current status quo, I need to be able to get them to use their imagination to visualise an ideal future state. I have lots of tools in my toolbox to support this process. But I will be working with a group of young adults who have two obstacles in their way. Firstly, their imaginations will have been saturated with negative future states. They will have had an entire lifetime of being told that the future is desperately awful, that there is no hope, and they will have pictures emblazoned on their brains of a dying world, concrete jungles devoid of nature, dead coral reefs and drowning refugees. It takes a lot to move beyond these images to find something new … but it is possible.

However — and this is the second obstacle — they will have had very little practice using their imaginations, because of the belief that play and the arts is a leisure activity and not a cognitive necessity. And what practice they have had was likely to have been very high stakes ("come up with a new future or we're all going to die").

I could still make it through all this if my group was willing to take a few intellectual and personal risks, to unlearn some of their existing assumptions, and to take a leap with me into the unknown.

But there are a few more things in their way.

Firstly, *not* taking risks will have become a habit. When they played at the playground, their parents told them how high to climb and when to stop. At school, they were focused on finding the right answers and getting the right grades and risk taking was discouraged. They will have been trained to go towards a definitive answer that an adult is leading them towards. They are unlikely to feel comfortable following their instincts towards an unknown answer and seeing where they end up. They may go through the motions of taking risks (possibly to please me, or to look good to their peers), but these risks are likely to be tentative and conservative.

And secondly, I can almost guarantee that their capacity to take risks will have been negatively impacted because they won't have a strong sense of belonging.

Whoa. Wait a minute. Belonging? What's that got to do with the science of innovation? It sounds more like something a liberal, artsy, baby-wearing hippy would go on about. Surely no self-respecting corporate team trying to innovate is going to get stuck on something as bizarre as belonging?

But, this, it turns out, is surprisingly important. From an evolutionary perspective, belonging to a group was literally a matter of life and death. As a result, our brains have learnt to take rejection as a physical assault, processed in the same way as physical pain. It sends us back into that survival mode, fighting for our lives, even when the stakes are nowhere near as high.

And a feeling of belonging is also crucial to being able to take a risk.

Most kids have spent a lot of time trying to 'fit in' and very little time actually belonging. Schools, on the whole, lay out a microcosm of society as a whole. And our cultural leaders — including our politicians, sports heroes, CEOs etc — regularly scorn people who don't fit, making comments that are racist or sexist or homophobic or disabled or ageist, or denigrating Indigenous communities or refugees or immigrants or even arts students. These comments don't just undermine the specific targets of the comments (which would be quite bad enough), but they also undermine everyone's potential for belonging. They send a message to everyone: "If you're different, you don't belong. You will be rejected and scorned."

And this baggage sits on the floor in the middle of an innovation workshop, like the proverbial elephant in the room. Only the most foolhardy among us would be stupid enough to blurt out a half-baked idea that nobody else has thought of if we care about fitting in. Risk taking, in this context, is inextricably linked to notions of belonging.

On the flipside, true belonging relies on difference, on genuine inclusivity and respect for diversity. Rather than making themselves small in order to fit in, ideally participants would be able to be the full extent of who they are without fear of judgment or reprisal. They can step into their strengths and preferences, knowing that the group is stronger because of its diversity. This is an unfamiliar experience for many people, especially those who have recently left school.

Diversity, in the context of innovation, also includes cognitive diversity — the understanding that our brains all work differently and that we have different strengths and preferences in thinking and the creative problem-solving process. If someone in the group is a *clarifier*, and naturally thinks of lots of questions to ask, their previous experiences of being told that they annoy people will likely make them ask only one or two of them. The others will never make it into the problem-solving process. Likewise, an *ideator* who has been criticised for taking up too much space will make their ideas more palatable and more aligned with everyone else's, which is devastating to the creative process, and will prevent genuine innovation.

Even worse, a culture of 'fitting in' rather than belonging is unlikely to yield emotionally intelligent responses to difficult questions. Many big hairy problems involve society's vulnerable and marginalised; a value of true belonging demands that teams bring compassion, empathy and ethics to their problem-solving, rather than ignoring or shunning those who 'don't fit.' This generates solutions which are 'large enough' to help everyone.

"But our kids do group work all the time!" I hear you cry. And it's true that a lot of schools do a lot of group work and collaboration. But being forced into a group for a school project does not foster a sense of belonging, and being dependent on other people for your grades does not foster empathy and compassion for people's differences.

Belonging, inclusivity and diversity then, are not wishy-washy liberal values that don't connect to the 'real world' — they are absolutely core to any kind of innovation.

And, finally, connected to this sense of belonging, is that effective group innovation demands some kind of commitment to a collective identity. The kinds of problems I tackle with teams are not able to be solved by a single individual, and they are not just for the benefit of a single individual. They are complex, multi-faceted issues that rely on a collectivist approach, for the mutual benefit of not only everyone in the room but for communities outside of it as well.

But Jamie, and her peers, have been raised in a society that puts individualism front and centre. They may do group work but ultimately they have been taught that their success depends on their 'individual effort.'

They will have been taught that individual issues are disconnected from systemic ones. If someone is unemployed, for example, it's because they haven't worked hard enough or they're lazy, not that economics relies on a certain unemployment rate. If a kid can't catch a ball, it's their fault, or their parents', and not because the local park has been developed into apartment blocks. If someone is sick, it's because they haven't 'looked after themselves,' and nothing to do with medical funding cuts.

And Jamie will also have been taught to look at social problems and respond to them as an individual. She will fight environmental problems by changing her light bulbs and using a recycling bin. She will fight corporate corruption by individually choosing not to buy a certain brand. She will fight back against the 'housing crisis' by personally saving money for a deposit (no smashed avocado for Jamie!).

Jamie will have been taught to respond to arguments about social trends with her own individual circumstances. *She* learnt the piano, so any argument about the decline of arts education in schools can't be valid. *She* was allowed to ride her bike to her friends' house so obviously any argument about freedom and risk taking is spurious. *She* put the hard work into getting into university, so arguments about inequalities in access to education are just excuses and not legitimate social concerns.

The force of these cultural influences make it difficult for people to think as groups and not individuals. Typically in a workshop, egos start to get in the way as participants vie for personal credit and ownership over ideas, as they struggle to see it as a collective effort. In addition, they will often struggle to conceptualise the needs of communities or groups that aren't represented in the room and will often fail to even recognise these communities as part of their own society. Yet for many complex issues, if we can only think of our own individual interests, our work is dead in the water before we even begin. Notions of collective identity are very difficult to teach in the moment if participants have no context for thinking that way.

So this is the group of Jamie and her peers who will be working with me to tackle the challenges of the future.

How do you think Jamie will do with all this?

Will she be able to throw off her desire to be a good student and know all the answers? Will she feel psychologically safe enough to throw ideas out there, to speak up for what she has to offer, to put herself on the edge and trust that her team has her back and will catch her? Will she find the wherewithal to navigate ambiguity and complexity? Will she have the emotional skills to help her peers to feel a deep sense of belonging so they can take creative risks? And will it even be possible to shift her neurological wiring out of survival mode into creative mode?

She might. It's true. Creativity is a science but a very unpredictable one and creativity has flourished in circumstances much worse than these. She might thrive.

But most likely, when she finds herself in this complex, ambiguous, space, being asked to apply ways of thinking for which she has very little training, looking for answers that don't yet exist … she will probably feel very unsafe and very uncertain and very unsure. She will probably tread carefully, make conservative choices about how much to give of herself, and need a lot of reassurance. She might even feel so unsafe that she leaves and doesn't come back.

At the very least, my work will be cut out for me, helping Jamie and her peers to unlearn some of their conditioning and assumptions and forging the conditions to allow them to be psychologically safe enough to take their first wobbly steps into the unknown.

Skills are easy to teach. I can teach brainstorming strategies, or how to develop a half-baked idea, or how to find the questions that are worth answering. I can teach skills. But I need a foundation to build on. I can't work with nothing.

It's not as bad as I make out, of course. The arts and humanities are not yet dead and, in fact, the business world is taking a renewed interest in them. Kids do still play and spend time outside. School isn't just about standardised testing, even if it sometimes feels like it is. And there are even signs that collectivisim is making a come-back.

But Jamie's story does give us food for thought. As we move into this unknown future that our kids will need to navigate with innovation and creativity, what is worth fighting for? What are we willing to do so that our kids can take on this creative work with confidence and strength?

We think that we're keeping our kids safe. But when we ignore their psychological safety, we aren't just taking them into a forest and asking them to look for five new things. We're dumping them in the middle of the wilderness, taking away their compasses, maps, GPS devices, tents, clothes, food and fire, reminding them that they are incapable and can't look after themselves, and then saying, cheerfully, "See you back at camp!"

This isn't setting them up for success.

Kids, like all humans, are naturally creative and, given the right support, they can grow into adults who are naturally creative. We just have to get out of their way.

Surely all *this* is worth fighting for?

Notes

1 I'm not saying that all of the tricky problems of the future will be solved in carefully designed innovation workshops. This is almost certainly not the case, but this is a thought experiment, so humour me.

2 In addition to, in all likelihood, a *lot* of screen time, probably since a young age, which also affects the brain, but that's a whole other debate.

3 Which is actually highly unlikely — Australia has one of the most socially segregated education systems in the world.

4 A previous Google study — Project Oxygen — examined the eight characteristics of the best managers. STEM skills came in at number eight. The top seven were all 'soft' skills that are usually fostered in the arts and humanities.

5 Like this one. Ahem.

References

Allen, K, Kern P & Waters, L 2018, 'Why Don't Australian School Kids Feel a Sense of Belonging?' *Pursuit* (University of Melbourne), 15 July, <https://pursuit.unimelb.edu.au/articles/why-don-t-australian-school-kids-feel-a-sense-of-belonging>.

Australian Council of Social Service 2018, *Poverty in Australia Report 2018*, ACOSS, Strawberry Hills, Australia,<https://www.acoss.org.au/wp-content/uploads/2018/10/ACOSS_Poverty-in-Australia-Report_Web-Final.pdf>.

Birss, D 2018, 'It's time to make workplace stress history,' *Open for Ideas*, 23 March, <http://openforideas.org/blog/2018/03/23/stress-kills-creativity-and-employees/>.

Blair, R 2014, 'How Stress Assassinates Creativity,' *Litreactor*, 10 April, <https://litreactor.com/columns/how-stress-assassinates-creativity>.

Brown, S L & Vaughan, C C 2009, *Play: how it shapes the brain, opens the imagination, and invigorates the soul*, Avery, New York.

Csikszentmihalyi, M 1991, *Flow: The Psychology of Optimal Experience*, Harper Collins, New York.

Delizonna, L 2017, 'High Performing Teams Need Psychological Safety. Here's How To Create It,' *HBR* [Harvard Business Review], 24 August, <https://hbr.org/2017/08/high-performing-teams-need-psychological-safety-heres-how-to-create-it>.

Duhigg, C 2016, 'What Google Learned From Its Quest to Build the Perfect Team,' *The New York Times Magazine*, 28 February, <https://www.nytimes.com/2016/02/28/magazine/what-google-learned-from-its-quest-to-build-the-perfect-team.html>.

Edmondson, A C 2018, *The Fearless Organization: Creating Psychological Safety in the Workplace for Learning, Innovation, and Growth*, John Wiley and Sons, New York.

Farr, T 2015, 'Standardization isn't Just Killing Students' Creativity', *Medium*, 11 November, <https://medium.com/synapse/standardization-isn-t-just-killing-students-creativity-3696a87ae391>.

Headspace, [n.d.], 'Majority of Aussie students stressed, depressed,' *Headspace*, <https://headspace.org.au/blog/majority-of-aussie-students-stressed-depressed/>.

Heinemeyer, C 2018, 'Mental health crisis in teens is being magnified by demise of creative subjects in school,' *The Conversation*, 3 September, <https://theconversation.com/mental-health-crisis-in-teens-is-being-magnified-by-demise-of-creative-subjects-in-school-102383>.

ICare & R U OK 2017, 'World-first study into workplace psychological safety launched,' *r u ok*, 29 May, <https://www.ruok.org.au/world-first-study-into-workplace-psychological-safety-launched>.

Jacobs R 2018, 'NAPLAN writing tests hinder creativity, so what could we use in their place?' *The Conversation*, 18 May, <https://theconversation.com/naplan-writing-tests-hinder-creativity-so-what-could-we-use-in-their-place-94735>.

Jensen, K 2018, 'Why Education Should Care About Psychological Safety,' *NeuroCapability*, <https://www.neurocapability.com.au/2018/04/education-care-psychological-safety/>.

McKay, J 2017, 'Workers are productive when they feel psychologically safe at work,' *Australian Financial Review*, 25 September, <https://www.afr.com/leadership/workers-are-productive-when-they-feel-psychologically-safe-at-work-20170925-gyo8zr>.

Menzies, F [n.d.], 'How to Develop Psychological Safety and a Speak Up Culture,' *CulturePlusConsulting*, <https://culturepulsconsulting.com/2018/03/10/how-to-develop-psychological-safety/>.

Puccio, G (ed.) 2014, *FourSight Thinking Profile: Interpretative Guide*, FourSight LLC, Evanston, Illinois, USA.

'Re:Work – Guide: Understand team effectiveness,' n.d., <https://rework.withgoogle.com/guides/understanding-team-effectiveness/steps/define-team/>.

Ricci, C 2015, 'Research shows cutting arts education a loss to all,' *The Age*, 2 March, <https://www.theage.com.au/education/research-shows-cutting-arts-education-a-loss-to-all-20150302-13sszl.html>.

Rosin, H 2014, 'The Overprotected Kid,' *The Atlantic*, April, <https://www.theatlantic.com/magazine/archive/2014/04/hey-parents-leave-those-kids-alone/358631/>.

Ruggeri, A 2019,'Why worthless humanities degrees may set you up for life,' *BBC Online*, 2 April, <http://www.bbc.com/capital/story/20190401-why-worthless-humanities-degrees-may-set-you-up-for-life>.

Shambaugh, R 2016, 'The Truth About Inclusion,' *Huffington Post*, <https://www.huffingtonpost.com/rebecca-shambaugh/the-truth-about-inclusion_b_11084352.html>.

Simpson, A [n.d.], 'Why an arts degree is now a must-have asset in the workplace,' *ArtsHub*, <https://www.artshub.com.au/education/news-article/sponsored-content/arts-education/andrea-simpson/why-an-arts-degree-is-now-a-must-have-asset-in-the-workplace-256988>.

Sutton-Smith, B 1997, *The Ambiguity of Play*, Harvard University Press, Cambridge, Mass.

Urban, R 2018, 'Students' stress levels up and confidence down,' *The Australian*, 15 June, <https://www.theaustralian.com.au/nation/education/students-stress-levels-up-and-confidence-down/news-story/7490651538721ba426314685f56ec3c1>.

Wheelahan D 2015, 'Nobel laureate urges young Australians to use creativity to solve world's pressing social problems,' *UNSW (Sydney) Newsroom*, 20 March, <https://newsroom.unsw.edu.au/news/health/nobel-laureate-urges-young-australians-use-creativity-solve-world's-pressing-social>.

Year 13, 2017, 'Results are In: Aussie High School Students are More Stressed than the Rest,' *Year 13*, 24 April, <https://year13.com.au/articles/results-aussie-high-school-students-stressed-rest>.

Leadership in children

Marilou Coombe

WHAT IS THE MEANING of *leadership*, especially when it comes to our children? Do most parents want their children to be leaders? How do we recognise leadership in our children? Is it a learned trait or are we born with it? What drives us to become great leaders? What are the qualities found in a leader? How can we help our children implement some of these traits? These are some of the aspects of leadership I would love to explore with you and share my perspective and experience thus far in this area.

I have worked with hundreds of children and the one thing I am certain of is that there is a leader in all of us, including the littlest humans. Whether that leadership trait flourishes or not depends on whether we are given the necessary skills and support. There are definitely those of us who are naturally charismatic and tend to draw people towards us. If we can harness and develop such characteristics, leadership is definitely achievable for everyone.

The dictionary defines *leadership* as the action of leading a group of people or an organisation; the state or position of being a leader; the leaders of an organisation, country, and so on. Although this is the traditional definition, we are starting to view it from a different perspective today. So many young people come to mind showing outstanding leadership. For example, Greta Thunberg, a 16-year-old Swedish activist, who is leading the fight on climate change, or Malala Yousafzai, a 22-year-old Pakistani activist for female education. What these young people have done in their own areas of passion is to lead great change and awareness on much needed topics. In the past we may not necessarily have thought of young people such as these being leaders, let alone bringing about much-needed changes into our world.

In my household it seems to be an important motivation for my young boys to be leaders. A simple question to check their behaviour is often "would a leader behave like that?" This gives them pause to think about how they want to behave and how that behaviour might be serving them. We are currently learning on how to be leading from *behind*, the *sides*, as well as the *front*. For young children this can be a difficult concept to comprehend.

I believe that great leaders are not always the ones leading and directing what others need to do. They give space and can help others to step into their own leadership roles, making room for anyone to step up and shine. They guide, encourage and cheer someone else's wins as if they were their own. This, I believe, is all learned behaviour because, generally speaking, our natural instinct as humans is to be competitive and egocentric.

So, what makes a great leader? There are a few traits I think we could talk about and encourage in our children when it comes to leadership:

Honesty and being congruent Owning up to mistakes and being sure what we say and how we act matches our words.

Confidence If you lack confidence and self-belief, others won't believe in you either. Confidence comes from the belief in what you do. It also grows by repeatedly doing the same thing and seeing the results of your effort.

Good communication When we can ask for what we want, direct others to what they need to do and use our words effectively, it can lead to being an outstanding leader.

Being committed When you show others that you too can get your hands dirty and do what you ask of others, you are more likely to gain their respect.

Capable of making decisions When asked to resolve something, being able to make a decision shows you are a leader not a follower.

Being accountable A good leader takes little more than his share of the blame and little less than his share of the credit. Holding self and others accountable for their words and actions. This also means when you commit to doing something by a certain time, you deliver by that deadline.

Delegation You can't do everything, so learning how to delegate to others is super helpful to being successful, and a top trait of a leader. Learning to say *no* is also a great skill to learn from an early age. When we say *yes* to everything, especially when we try to make others happy, we spread ourselves thin and are unable to complete tasks to their full potential.

Creative and visionary Seeing the bigger picture and taking different approaches to finding solutions. A leader doesn't merely demonstrate this in themselves, but also encourages it in others.

Empathy Showing how you care for someone through kindness and understanding, not as a 'fixer,' but rather to empower others so they can feel strong within themselves. It is important to distinguish between empathy and sympathy here, as empathy holds space for others to work through their own stuff and come up with their own solutions to a problem, rather than joining in with their problem and trying to fix it for them.

Inclusivity Helping them recognise how to include others in their thinking process. This is so crucial to learn from a young age, as we are wired as human to be egocentric and think about everything from our own perspective, rather than include others and consider their views, opinions and feelings.

Inspire others Being a great role model and doing what you expect of others. If your child wants people to speak nicely to them, teach them to do it first to others. It is so easy to ask of others before we act it ourselves.

Looks like an overwhelming list? Not really! The best way to teach these things is for we parents to model these qualities in our own lives. How often are we honest with ourselves as well as others? Are we accountable for our behaviours? This is a lot to think about, but with practice and dedication it is completely possible. What I see today are parents wanting things for their children because they either wanted it for themselves in their life but, for one reason or another, could not not obtain it. Or they think this is the way their child would be successful in life, but the parent does not display those same qualities in themselves. It is imperative to understand we are our children's best teachers and the best way to bring any quality out in our children is to master it within us.

So how can you bring about these leadership qualities in your child? As a family, we have done a few things on the list below and they seem to really have helped. As my children grow older, I am sure there will also be other strategies we will offer.

Support their ideas If your child wants to write a book, create art, play football all day, then support them where and when possible. Children thrive best and are driven, like adults, when they love what they do, and especially if it was their own idea in the first place. Understanding their values and how to motivate children by allowing them to do what they love is the most important way to awaken the leader in any child. My boys love sports, football in particular. They draw about it, create shows about it and it is what they speak about the most. Supporting them in this, allows them to grow and build thought processes around a particular interest, which they will be able to apply when they move on to other interests.

Encourage team activity Identifying what sparks your child's interest and encouraging them to partake in an activity to support this interest will allow your child to blossom and take on different roles within a team environment. This strategy is so helpful as they learn how to lead from all different aspects as outlined above, not necessarily by telling everyone what to do. With our children being involved with a football team and a karate centre, the responsibilities they have been given have truly shaped them to be great leaders in their interaction with others. This has been especially evident with my eldest son who has had to work hard on his confidence and communication skills.

Play board games and other family games together Teaching a child how to lose gracefully is equally as important as winning. We can guide them about their attitude, team effort, game spirit, and handling 'failure' in a safe environment while supporting their feelings. Losing for a child can be really hard and tantrums in our household occur frequently. When winning has been the focus, traits such as cheating can creep in. This is a great opportunity for we parents to discuss with them the choices they make and how does it really benefit them. We have a saying at home that "cheaters will always be losers even if they win." They know the truth and that is all that matters. If they know they did not win by effort and strategy, they also know they will not be able to improve those skills if the win is only superficial.

Teach them to earn their allowance Nothing increases leadership skills as well as creativity at the same time as encouraging children to earn their money to purchase what they want. My children rarely get a toy they want without having to think how they will earn it. This encourages creativity, resourcefulness and commitment. If they really want it, they will make it happen. And when this is aligned with their highest value, they sure do. This includes purchase of *Lego* sets or outings to special places they want to experience. They have sold their own toys, created bookmarks to sell, made lists of chores to get paid for and learned to negotiate in order to get what was important to them.

Step back This is perhaps one of the hardest ones to do as we parents want to do so much for our children. Unconsciously we hinder their abilities to be able to do things for themselves. This could be as trivial as letting a two-year-old help load a washing machine to a teen making their own way to school. When we step back and allow them to give things a go, their confidence and analytical skills grow. I have witnessed this in my household when I was running late in making lunches and my eight-year-old stepped up and made sandwiches for both himself and brother. The pride he felt at his achievement was evident on his face and the way he told his dad about it. I have become aware of how much we do for our children that we should allow them to do for themselves and for which they are more than capable.

Allow them to find their own conflict resolution This is evident with siblings or during conflict with other family members. Rather than stepping in with a solution or separating the parties, allow them to talk it through and find a result that will make everyone happy. When my children fight each other and run to try and to get their sibling in trouble, unless there is a broken body part or blood, I decline to get involved. They have to sort it out and come back to me speaking calmly if they need me still. Nine out of ten times, they have sorted it out. In turn, they have become quite great negotiators and solution finders.

Ask questions Have the conversations with your child where you ask open ended questions about certain topics challenging them presently. Challenge their views and have them thinking about why they have these thoughts and views. And accept it may be different to your own thinking. In our family, we are trying to manage our consumerist behaviours and are rethinking many of our purchases in categories of needs and wants. It has become important to reduce the stuff we accumulate thinking we need it but really it is only because we want it. So, when our children want the latest gadgets that their friends have, we ask them "why?" How does it enhance their life by having it? Are there other ways they can obtain it? Is there evidence of other toys bought and now no longer looked at? It has them thinking about their own choices and how it may affect the environment and our life. So much so, that my eldest was picked as school environment captain due to his speech on supporting the planet and how we can do our part. Most of it was his own words and thinking, without my input.

Accept and deal with the negative as well as the positive When we make space for our children's emotions, the sad and happy ones, we encourage them to be more balanced with their views of themselves and the world. We teach them not to hold things which can manifest undesired outcomes later in life. Aiming for a world of only positivity is what creates anxiety and the need to look for approval from outside sources for our feelings.

Acknowledging that the world exists with both negative and positive experiences and emotions allows our children to cultivate stronger inner compasses. I recently had a student tell me they made a pact with their mother that they would only say and think positive things. I asked them how they would do that when negative situations arose — and if they are only to think positively, how would they know it was positive if they did not have the negative to compare it to? Certainly, we want our offspring to be kind, speak nicely, think positively about themselves, yet it is not humanly possible to do this consistently. Learning that a negative situation arises to show us how to adjust and pay attention to something that is not working for us is a much healthier perspective.

Recently I asked a group of young people, aged 14-19 years, for their definition of leadership and what it means to them. I think it is especially important to understand what a certain concept means to somebody else, so we don't overlay our own values, expectations and perceptions on to them. That is the sure recipe for conflict and a sense of failure on the parties involved. I love their answers.

I asked this particular group because I already view them as leaders in their own right — each and every single one of them. They show up to a yearly summit, get vulnerable with their feelings, face fears and learn new skills that they apply in real world situations. Then they utilise their new learnings and share it with other young people to empower them to be their best. Their answers to my question reflect this:

Cheyenne: "Leadership means when someone is taking action in what they strongly believe in and that they are an independent and strong minded individual, leadership is a positive and support act of kindness."

Tiana: "Leadership is being able to make a difference in the lives of others. We all have different experiences and each leader has something others don't. I think being a leader means being understanding, empathetic and able to listen to and support others."

Hannah: "Good leaders are able to speak up about their own ideas and opinions while still listening to those of others. They are able to compromise and make decisions for the benefit of others, and work as a fair team member. Being a leader means to be proactive with your decisions and your overall life (e.g. school assignments) and taking initiative when others will not. I believe that good leaders are passionate about their goals and dreams, and have determination and perseverance to achieve them, even though they know that it will not be easy. A leader needs to have good communication skills and be kind and considerate to all, as well as have the ability to understand others' perspectives and have empathy towards them. Leaders should not see their job as a burden, but as an opportunity to help others."

Nathan: "A leader is someone who's actions inspire others to dream more, learn more, do more or become more."

Wil: "A leader is about being the same person and having the ownership and integrity to be that person you are with people around as you would be with no one around."

These young humans are creating magic in their own small and big ways, inspiring and leading others to do the same. You can see in their own words that they are incorporating some of my suggestions into their leadership skill base. I also know they are getting the support they need from others around them to show up and be their best in leading others.

Remember, there are no perfect humans. Many great leaders have their downsides as well as their great qualities. And if we accept people as a whole package of polarity and duality, especially our children, we can direct them to be their amazing selves, leading us into a promising and hopeful future. And with us, as parents and carers, focused on our own leadership qualities, we can inspire those around us to do the same, especially our children.

14

Responsibility parenting

Andrew Lines

FOR THE LAST 25 YEARS I have spent my life surrounded by children and young people — my own four children, three step-sons and thousands of students who have crossed my path in my role as a teacher. Over time I have noticed that the nature of parenting has changed creating a distinct shift in the experience for children and young people compared to how things were when I was a child.

In recent years there has been a spate of parenting books written focusing on raising 'Gen Alpha' children. Titles such as 'Spoonfed Generation', 'Escaping the Endless Adolescence,' 'The Collapse of Parenting,' 'The Gift of Failure' and subtitles such as 'How the quest for success is harming our kids,' 'Break free of the over-parenting trap and prepare your kid for success,' 'How to step back and let your child succeed.' These titles all reflect a generation of parents who have been given various labels: Helicopter Parents, Lawnmower Parents, Snowplough Parents, and in Denmark — Curling Parents.

Parenting today largely appears to be aimed at keeping our children happy, making their lives easy and offering them every opportunity for success. However, a recent publication suggests that we might not be going about it the right way.

In their book *The Happiest Kids in the World — Bringing up children the Dutch Way*, Rina Mae Acosta and Michele Hutchison (2018, p. 283) discuss the fact that research shows Dutch teenagers are the happiest in the world. When they quizzed Professor Ruut Veenhoven (aka the Happiness Professor) of Rotterdam's Erasmus University as to why this was the case he "put it down to there being a higher degree of 'independence training' in the Netherlands. Kids have more freedom and are less overprotected than in other countries."

So maybe the current above-mentioned parenting styles aren't actually the best way to create 'happy' teenagers. In fact, the most recent *Mission Australia Youth Survey* found that the percentage of young people identifying mental health as an issue of national importance has doubled in the last three years from 21 percent to 43 percent:

> The top three issues of concern for young people were coping with stress, school or study problems and mental health. Compared to the results from previous years, the top two issues of personal concern remain unchanged, while mental health was ranked as the third most-reported issue of personal concern for the first time. (*Mission Australia Youth Survey Report*, 2018, p. 23)

It seems that in our endeavour to ensure that our children grow up happy with good 'self esteem' we may have been creating children who have been referred to as anxious, 'wusses,' lacking resilience and entitled. The responsibility for the state of a culture or society lies with its elders and so I felt a responsibility as a parent and teacher to address what I was hearing.

Initially I pondered the differences between the experience of my own childhood and that of my children. And whilst I acknowledge that most generations seem to lament the state of the following generation (there is even a Socrates quote in which he complains of the disrespect of the youth of his day) I observe that the world that my children are growing up in is vastly different from what I experienced as a child.

During my parent sessions I often ask the question "How is the experience of your child different from that of your own childhood?" The most common responses include access to technology, social media, freedom and less risk.

In hearing parents' responses over the years I have been moved to consider how we might address these differences so that we can make a change to our own parenting. When I have further explored what issues parents raise a number of points seem to stand out.

Firstly, adults seem to suggest that there was more time spent together as a family. For instance people often comment about mealtimes being a moment of togetherness without too much disruption. An opportunity to discuss the day's events and check in on how each member of the family is.

Then there is often a comment about the freedom of outdoor play. Almost always someone talks about hopping on their bike in the morning and riding off for the day … with the only instruction being "make sure you're home by dinner!" People reflect on the feeling of freedom they had in those moments and the necessity of self-reliance if anything arose during their day out.

Another issue that adults note has come about due to advances in technology is immediate access to a host of information and entertainment. For instance, the ability to instantly *Google* answers has transformed us from a 'question rich, answer poor' society to a 'question poor, answer rich' society. The advent of *Netflix* has meant that we no longer need to wait one week for the next instalment of our favourite tv series. In this era of instant gratification how do we teach our children the skill of delayed gratification — one of life's key learnings, as M Scott Peck suggests in *The Road Less Travelled* (1978, p. 19) "the only decent way to live"?

As a child I remember having a lot more connection with adults than I see with my children. Whenever I wanted to call a friend it was typically their parent who answered the phone. This led to a sometimes awkward chat where I was required to put on my 'adult hat' to conduct a conversation with an adult. In the world of mobile phones there is almost no need for young people to communicate with friends' parents as they have direct access via a device. I believe that moments where children are required to access their 'higher self' to conduct a respectful conversation with an adult are a cornerstone for building their communication skills.

An important task for parents is to equip our children with the necessary skills for adulthood. This includes enabling them to be able to deal with challenges, risks and failure. The perfect opportunity to foster learning for our children in these areas is in small stakes situations that arise throughout childhood and young adulthood.

However, in today's world there is a tendency to protect children from risk. A simple exercise to explore this is to compare an old school trampoline to the current incarnation. What you will see is the modern day trampoline completely surrounded by a net, whereas the old school trampoline has no net and more often than not were *sans* padding.

An essential part of childhood is learning to assess risks but in our sanitised play environments our children are denied that opportunity. Trampolining is not high stakes risk — but every jump on an un-netted trampoline requires a little risk assessment: "Am I still in the middle?" To deny a child the opportunity to learn the skills and nuances of risk assessment in 'small stakes' situations during play denies them the opportunity to learn resilience, resourcefulness and problem solving for the years ahead.

I would prefer my child learns these skills at six, seven or eight years of age, in my backyard — than the first time they experience needing to make risk assessments is at the age of 17 years driving on the roads — in an situation where I won't be nearby to help them out.

I recently received a delightful message of thanks from a parent:

Dear Andrew,
Eons ago, I heard you speak about risk, and teaching children to calculate risks at age appropriate stages. I remember the images of the trampolines you had side by side and how you explained that if children don't learn to evaluate the risk of jumping on a trampoline, how would they ever drive a car safely. Today, I took my kids (6 and 8) cycling on the road for the first time. My heart was in my feet the entire time, especially as I watched them wobble ... but I just thought about all the risks I was safely introducing them to and continued to ride behind and alongside them. When we got home they were grinning and giggling and so proud of themselves. So, thank you. For all that your program has taught me as a teacher and as a parent.

As an aside I was once challenged by a parent about not wanting kids to break bones etc. So I did some research and guess what I discovered — the advent of nets on trampolines hasn't necessarily reduced the number of injuries on trampolines, rather it has just changed the nature of the injuries.

These days it sees situations like 90kg dads feeling safe jumping around inside a netted trampoline with their child leading to significant injuries with dads landing on their children. Bones are still broken — just in other ways.

Small stakes opportunities to teach our children important life lessons come around regularly. According to a report in *The Australian* newspaper, Australian psychologist Michael Carr-Gregg is concerned about our tendency to protect kids from such lessons:

> Parents shield their children from any negativity so that when life confronts them, they are completely incapable of dealing with loss, grief or stress … A distraught mother once phoned Carr-Gregg when her son's goldfish died. "Should I buy another one that looks the same?" she asked. "One day you'll be that goldfish," Carr-Gregg replied. "You need to teach your child to deal with grief." (Bita, 2016)

As parents we should be embracing the small stakes opportunities to teach our children valuable lessons.

When reflecting on my experience of school I can remember receiving an end of semester report with one or two unsatisfactory results. I felt great trepidation with the thought of handing the report card over to my parents. I knew that they would hold me accountable for my performance that semester. They would ask me what I was going to do to improve my grade. As teachers, what we notice happens these days is that rather than parents holding their child accountable for any poor grades, they tend to hold the teacher responsible for their child's grade.

This kind of response is an example to the child of blame and not taking responsibility. They learn to play the victim. And we wonder where the sense of entitlement in young people comes from!

> We cannot solve life's problems except by solving them … This is because we must accept responsibility for a problem before we can solve it. We cannot solve a problem by saying "It's not my problem." (Peck, 1978, p. 32).

When we consider the age of responsibility and dependence, historically the transition from child to adult in most cultures happened somewhere between 12 and 15-years-of-age. Typically an individual was either considered a child or an adult.

In traditional cultures there were significant moments throughout life, especially Rites of Passage, which were celebrated with ceremony. Five of these stages which were typically honoured throughout the life-cycle were birth, child to adult transition, marriage, adult to elder transition and death. In our current western culture we still tend to celebrate births, deaths and marriages. We have lost the rites of marking the transitions from child to adult and adult to elder.

Traditional initiations usually included an education in being an adult in that particular society. This would be some kind of challenge, usually one that was physical in nature, honouring the individual and then the expectation that they take their place in adult society, and step into responsibility.

However, this concept has become more complex in recent years with the advent of adolescence. In 1904, G Stanley Hall, the then American Psychological Association president, was credited with discovering adolescence (Henig, 2010). He wrote a study on 'Adolescence,' in which he described this new phase which had arisen due to social changes in the early 1900s. Further work and understanding of this stage came about in the 1950s.

Initially this transitional phase of adolescence was only deemed to be a two or three year period but in the last half a century it has grown to stretch between nine and 26-years-of-age, a span of 17 years. I would like to think that we can expect young people to step responsibly into adulthood much younger than 26 years.

In Australia, the legal age of criminal responsibility is ten years. However the age of adulthood when an individual has the same legal rights as an adult is 18 years. It is at this point that each 'child' lands on a level legal playing field with their parents. Given the shift in childhood and the way we parent I have a real concern with how well we have prepared our children to cross over this threshold.

Young people yearn to have such a process and tend to create the experiences themselves if the elders in their culture don't. Processes such as 'schoolies week' here in Australia and 'hazing' at colleges and universities in the United States are young people's attempt to create such a transitional process themselves. I firmly believe that it is time we rediscovered these transitions in a contemporary way.

Ultimately the state of any society or culture is the responsibility of its elders and I believe we, the adults, need to step up and be doing a better job of creating young adults.

Given the state of play at the moment regarding the experience of young people in the twenty-first century, the common parenting styles and the lack of rites of passage, I suggest that we can create a far more structured and planned approach to building responsibility, resilience, and resourcefulness as well as honouring the transition of our children into young adulthood.

I propose a 'Parenting Plan' or a 'Transition Template' which has a scaffold of increasing responsibility as well as rituals throughout childhood where we honour and celebrate the significant transition points with an aim to have created a responsible, resourceful, respectful and resilient adult by the time they are 18-years-old.

I believe that using birthdays as the basis for these transition points is the perfect opportunity to both add a new responsibility to their life in the family and also to gift them relevant, useful presents that echo that particular responsibility.

Henri Nouwen's poem offers a delightful perspective as the backdrop for these birthday transition points:

> Birthdays need to be celebrated. I think it is more important to celebrate a birthday than a successful exam, a promotion, or a victory. Because to celebrate a birthday means to say to someone: "Thank you for being you." Celebrating a birthday is exalting life and being glad for it. On a birthday we do not say: "Thanks for what you did, or said, or accomplished." No, we say: "Thank you for being born and being among us." On birthdays we celebrate the present. We do not complain about what happened or speculate about what will happen, but we lift someone up and let everyone say: "We love you." (Nouwen, 2019)

A key starting point for creating our own Parenting Plan is to be intentional in establishing our family culture. To spend some time deciding which values, rituals and behaviours we'd like to have as hallmarks of our family life that will build connection and foster responsibility, resilience, reverence and respect.

A great place to start is by creating some family rituals. These can be daily or weekly. Children thrive on familiarity and rhythm. Find a couple of things that become daily rituals and a couple of things that are regular weekly experiences with the children.

Possible daily rituals might include:
- a morning walk — this might be as a family or just with one child and shared around during the various walking days
- sitting down for an afternoon snack together
- no technology hour
- all eating dinner together
- lighting a candle for dinner
- saying a blessing before a meal
- sharing a story about your day at the dinner table (no mobile phones)
- a story before bedtime
- sharing three points of gratitude at the end of the day
- a bedtime song, blessing or prayer

Possible weekly or fortnightly rituals might include:
- games night
- movie night
- a meal cooked by a child
- visiting the grandparents
- playing in the park
- a regular takeaway meal night
- music or art evening
- visit an elderly neighbour
- sports afternoon
- no technology day

Other rituals might include:
- acknowledging the new season
- family celebrations
- camping trips
- family holidays
- Religious traditions and celebrations
- Birthday celebrations

Birthdays are a wonderful opportunity to individually honour each child just for who they are. I think it is well worth spending some time considering how you'd like birthdays to look in your home. You might choose to tell the birth story in the morning upon waking, the table could be set beautifully and the room decorated with balloons and streamers. You could create a special birthday 'throne' and the birthday child may get to choose what's for breakfast.

Each of my children had a special birthday candle which would only be placed on the table and lit on their birthday but for the rest of the year it sits on the sideboard as a visual reminder of their birth.

A birthday is also effectively a graduation into the next year of life and an opportunity to not only honour your child but to also graduate them in responsibility.

I suggest that as parents we create a birthday template which includes both an intentional gift and a new responsibility around the house. Rather than purchasing our child the 'next shiny new toy,' we will give them worthwhile, memorable, usable gifts which reflect the next stage of responsibility we are encouraging them to step up into.

Below is a sample template with suggestions as to the various gifts, responsibilities and experiences that I think would work well from ages two to 18 years. It is intended as a guide and each family should carefully consider what they feel would be appropriate for their own children.

Two-years-old "I tidy my bedroom."

Gift — Toy box, toys, book case, books.

Responsibility — Tidying their room before bed each evening.

Three-years-old "I make my bed."
Gift — Nice bedding, quilt, pillow, pyjamas.
Responsibility — Making their bed each morning, folding their pyjamas and placing them under their pillow.

Four-years-old "I play outside, by myself."
Gift — Outside play equipment: ropes course, swing, sandpit, cubby house, tree house, swing set.
Responsibility — Spending time playing outside, sometimes unsupervised.
Experience — A trip to an adventure playground.

Five-years-old "I organise myself to go to school. I'm creative."
Gift — School bag, drink bottle, lunch box, coloured pencil set/crayons/paints, jigsaw.
Responsibility — Organising themselves in the morning, including making breakfast and getting out of the door.
Experience — A trip to the local art gallery and/or theatre for an introduction to the arts.

Six-years-old "I ride on wheels on the road. I play sport."
Gift — Two wheeler bike, billycart, scooter, sports gear, sports membership
Responsibility — Riding on the road.
Experience — A trip to a bike track and to a sporting event.

Seven-years-old "I care for the environment. I'm learning about money."
Gift — Gardening set, voucher for seedlings/fruit tree, vegetable patch, 3 x money boxes (give, save, spend), money.
Responsibility — Looking after plants in the garden. Learning about money: saving, giving, spending.
Experience — A trip to the plant nursery to select seedlings/fruit tree.

Eight-years-old "I care for animals. I move further afield."
Gift — Pet: gold fish, guinea pig, chickens, budgie, cat, etc., walkie talkie.
Responsibility — Caring for an animal. Being further away from parents and home.
Experience — Trip to a wildlife park or zoo. Volunteering at RSPCA.

Nine-years-old "I'm self-reliant."
Gift — Sleeping bag, small tent, pocket knife, survival guide.
Responsibility — Setting up and packing up tent, using a knife, making school lunches.
Experience — A camping evening in the backyard with friends.

10-years-old "I'm organised and in charge of my time."
Gift — A watch and an alarm clock.
Responsibility — Being solely responsible for waking up and being timely.
Experience — Child plans a family day in the city including using public transport timetable, organising lunch etc.

11-years-old "I choose my own clothes and take care of them."
Gift — Sewing machine, sewing kit, clothes voucher, clothes basket.
Responsibility — Learn to sew and fix clothing (buttons/holes in socks etc), learn to iron, learn to use the washing machine and wash own clothes, choose own clothes.
Experience — A trip to the clothing store to buy own clothes.

12-years-old "I can travel on my own."
Gift — Interstate trip by themselves (to visit relatives / friends), movie vouchers.
Responsibility — Being away from home by themselves.
Experience — A day to the city for a movie by themselves or just with friends.

13-years-old "I can cook and look after myself."
Gift — Camp cooker, electric cooking appliance (pizza maker, ice cream maker, hot dog maker etc), cookbook with favourite recipes of friends and extended family, first aid kit.
Responsibility — Make an evening meal for the family once a fortnight.
Experience — A cooking class.

14-years-old "I am independent. I am social. I can budget."
Gift — Bank account including an amount deposited per month, finance book (*Barefoot Investor*), swag, mobile phone (loaned).
Responsibility — Paying for toiletries, underwear and mobile phone plan.
Experience — Camping out solo.

15-years-old "I take responsibility for my things and relationships and fix them when required."
Gift — Tool set, personal development book, adult bike.
Responsibility — Take care of and be responsible for their own things and their relationships.
Experience — Personal development course.

16-years-old "I present well. I am a responsible road user. I am a responsible phone user."
Gift — Fragrance, shaving set, make up, an evening outfit that they choose, driving lessons, own phone.
Responsibility — Self-care, presenting well and a responsible driver and communicator.
Experience — Interstate family holiday with them driving.

17-years-old "I am financially responsible."
Gift — Stylish purse/wallet, increased allowance into bank account, defensive driving course.
Responsibility — Expected to buy all clothing, recreation and treats.
Experience — Financial literacy course.

18-years-old "I am responsible."

Gift — Hip flask, wine tasting course, travelling backpack, suit/evening dress, RM Williams boots.

Responsibility — Being responsible for self and others beyond 18 years.

Experience — A meaningful trip away instead of 'schoolies.'

Another possible consideration for each age, to help our children understand the link between freedom and responsibility, could be to consider an age-appropriate freedom that they can step into as well. On occasions this may simply be going to bed a little bit later than the previous year or being able to go a little further away from home on their bike. The purpose of the template of gifts, responsibilities and freedoms is to gradually grow a responsible, respectful, resilient and resourceful young person who, by the time they turn 18 years, is ready to leave the nest.

As well as using the responsibilities template I suggest that we celebrate some other significant moments throughout our child's life. I suggest we have a number of formal Rites of Passage with our children:

Menarche This is the opportunity to celebrate with our daughters their first period. This Rite of Passage is generally overseen by women and involves other women. A great resource to assist in this process is 'A Blessing Not a Curse' by Jane Bennett.

Boy to Man, Girl to Woman The child to adult Rite of Passage is a process in which the boys' initiation was overseen by the men and the girls' by the women. The process generally happened around 14-years-of-age. In 1909 anthropologist Arnold Van Gennep recognised that most cultures transitioned individuals from one social role to another by way of what he termed 'rites of passage'. He recognised three distinct elements throughout different cultures: separation, transformation and reincorporation. (Van Gennep, 1904)

Richard Rohr in his book *Adam's Return: The Five Promises of Male Initiation* summarises what he sees as the five truths of adulthood: life is hard, you are not in control, life is not about you, you are not that important and you are going to die. (Rohr, 2004) The importance of transitioning from child psychology to adult psychology is an important element of this child to adult Rite of Passage.

M Scott Peck in *The Road Less Travelled* acknowledged a similar truth:

> Life is difficult.
> This is a great truth, one of the greatest truths. It is a great truth because once we see this truth, we transcend it. Once we truly know that life is difficult — once we truly understand and accept it — then life is no longer difficult. Because once it is accepted, the fact that life is difficult no longer matters. (Peck 1978, p. 15)

A core part of my own work over the past 20 years has been to develop a school-based year long Rite of Passage process called *The Rite Journey* which acknowledges the lack of an initiation process into adulthood in western culture. The *Rite Journey* expands the aforementioned three elements that Van Gennep recognised into a seven stage transition process from adolescence into adulthood using the archetype of a Hero's Journey.

The Hero's Journey was coined by Joseph Campbell in his 1949 book *The Hero with a Thousand Faces*. He was an author and teacher with an interest in mythology who analysed stories, fables and legends from all over the world and discovered within them distinct similarities in their structure. He also recognised the connection between Van Gennep's observations of adolescent into adulthood rites from around the world. Campbell renamed Van Gennep's three elements, calling them Departure, Initiation and Return and within these three he identified a series of up to 15 stages that typified a hero's journey.

The Rite Journey distils his findings into seven key stages — The Calling, The Departure, The Following, The Challenges, The Abyss, The Return and The Homecoming:

> **The Calling** At a significant local landmark the students show gratitude for their childhood and are called on their journey to adulthood.

The Departure Parents, carers and mentors join the students for an opportunity to reflect, learn and look forward.

The Following The students are guided throughout the year by a number of supportive adults including teachers, parents/carers and mentors.

The Challenges Resilience is built by giving students challenges and helping them acquire the skills, resources and mindset necessary to overcome them.

The Abyss The biggest challenge of the year takes students out of their comfort zone to help them learn more about themselves.

The Return Students reflect on what they have learned and experienced during the year and acknowledge the gifts and skills they will carry into adulthood.

The Homecoming Students are celebrated and honoured at a gratitude ceremony involving teachers, parents/ carers and mentors.

Along with the *The Rite Journey* Framework is a series of close to 100 conversations throughout the year. They cover the following four themes:

Who am I really? Students gain an understanding of themselves by exploring self-identity and the expectations placed on them by society. Topics include gender identity, self-awareness and body image.

How do I get along with others? This theme assists students in exploring their role in relationships. Conversations include emotional literacy, listening, non-violence, anger management and healthy sexuality.

Is there something more? Throughout this unit students reflect on some of the deeper aspects of life including stillness, mindfulness, values, sadness, happiness, mortality and wisdom.

What do I have to give? The final theme prompts students to consider their future, what they have to offer the world and calls them to responsibility. Topics include leadership, intentions, kindness and gratitude.

I have also conducted this process, individually with each of my own sons. We spent a few weeks away and used both the seven stages and the four conversation themes to usher them from childhood into young adulthood. I now offer workshops for men who would like to offer a similar process for the boy in their life.

I suggest that parents either source an organisation that offers a Rite of Passage process for their child or undergo some training so that they have a template to use themselves. I have created a number of resources to assist parents in this process including *Man Made Conversation Cards* and *Woman Wise Conversation Cards*.

This Rite of Passage is perhaps the most important point in an individual's life, as they move from child to adult. Helping young people go through this process has become my life's work and I encourage dads to explore how you might do this with your boys and mums how you might do it with your girls.

The final Rite of Passage of childhood I call *The Release*. This process occurs on an individual's 18th birthday and acknowledges their step into independent adulthood and our 'step back', as parents. It is an intentional moment in which we acknowledge to our 18-year-old that they are now an adult and legally have the same place as us, their parents. I let my child know that I will be making a conscious effort from now on to enable them to develop into their own person, that I won't choose to force my opinions or thoughts onto them any longer but, of course, will always be there for them should they like to seek out my opinion or advice.

It is an empowering gesture that provides them with space to grow rather than restricting them or causing them to be overly worried about pleasing their parent(s). I let them know that a part of life is making mistakes and failing and that I will always be there to support them but will not be preventing their learning by rescuing them. It is also a choice to own 'our stuff' as parents and not to burden our adult children with it.

There are a number of ways that such a moment might look like but two important elements of the process are some form of public declaration of our intention and a token of the moment.

A final element of this *Release* process I undertook with my newly 18-year-old is to attend a couple of therapy sessions with them in which I ask them to share with me any issues they have had with my fathering over the years. I wanted them to tell me when they have felt unsupported, let down, ignored etc. I wanted them to have the opportunity to clear the air with me simply reflectively listening to them. It was a difficult process but one that I felt released ongoing resentments or 'skeletons in the closet.' It felt like a cleansing and cleared the path for our ongoing relationship in its new incarnation as two adults.

Being a parent in the twenty-first century is a complex task. We are raising children in a very different world to that in which we grew up and there is a pressure to create a happy and carefree life for our children. However, it appears our children are less resilient and more anxious than ever.

I believe that if we make a conscious effort to have a considered parenting plan that we will be able to develop young adults who, having turned 18 years, will be responsible, resilient, resourceful and respectful.

References

Acosta, R M, Hutchinson, M 2018 *The Happiest Kids in the World : Bringing up children the Dutch Way*, Transworld Publishers, London.

Allen, J, Allen, C W 2009, *Escaping the Endless Adolescence: How We Can Help Our Teenagers Grow Up Before They Grow Old*, Ballantine Books, New York.

Bennett, J 2002 *A Blessing Not a Curse: A Mother-Daughter Guide to the Transition from Child to Woman*, Sally Milner Publishing, Binda, NSW.

Bita, N 2016 'Kids are sponges for bad parenting,' *The Australian*, 30 April, <https://www.theaustralian.com.au/nation/inquirer/kids-are-sponges-for-bad-parenting/news-story/>.

Campbell, J 1949, *The Hero with a Thousand Faces*, Pantheon Books, New York.

Carlisle, E, Fildes, J, Hall, S, Hicking, et al 2018, *Youth Survey Report 2018*, Mission Australia, Sydney.

Clark, L 2017, *Beautiful failures: how the quest for success is harming our kids*, Penguin Random House, North Sydney, NSW.

Grose, M 2017, *Spoonfed Generation: How to raise independent children*, Transworld Publishers, Milson's Point, NSW.

Henig, R M 2010, 'What is it about 20-somethings? Why are so many people in their 20s taking so long to grow up?' *The New York Times Magazine*, 22 October 2010, <http://www.nytimes.com/2010/08/22/magazine/22Adulthood-t.html?>.

Lahey, J 2015, *The Gift of Failure: How to step back and let your child succeed*, Harper Collins, New York.

Lythcott-Haims, J 2016, *How to Raise an Adult : Break Free of the Overparenting Trap and Prepare Your Kid for Success*, Henry Holt and Co, London.

Nouwen, H 2019, *Birthday*, <https://henrinouwen.org/meditation/birthdays/>.

Peck, M S 1978, *The Road Less Travelled*, Simon and Schuster, New York.

Rohr, R 2004, *Adam's Return: The Five Promises of Male Initiation*, Crossroads, New York.

Sax, L 2016, *The Collapse of Parenting: How we hurt our kids when we treat them like grown-ups*, Basic Books, New York.

Van Gennep, A 1960/2004, *Les Rites de Passage*, first published 1960, reprinted 2004, Routledge, London.

Index

Aboriginal and Torres Strait Islander Peoples 41
Aboriginal Australians, connection to land 113-115
ADHD (Attention Deficit Hyperactivity Disorder) 44
adolescence 14, 17-18, 22, 163, 171,
AFLW (Australian Football League Women) 120
American Psychological Association 163
APS disaster resources 18
Asperger's [Syndrome] 85
Attenborough, David 4
Australian Association for Infant Mental Health Inc. 63
Australian Parents for Climate Action x, 3, 9,
Australian Psychological Society x, 3, 4

Biddulph, Steve xii, 4, 55,
birthing 70-71
Black History 107, 110
Carr-Greg, Michael 162
Citizens Climate Lobby 3
civic engagement 22
Civil War, American 107-108
clarifier 142
climate consciousness, transition to 27-28
Climate Emergency Declaration 3
congruence 81-82, 86
consumerism, quitting 35-36
coping, distress of climate change 12-13, 19-20
creativity, in play 134-136
Cripps, Elizabeth 16
Cuban Missile Crisis 51
diet 31, 115
eco-anxiety 33

education, role of   56-58, 64, 89, 95, 113
Eisenstein, Charles   vii, viii, 69, 74,
el-Shabazz, Malik (Malcolm X)   8
electromagnetic field   78-79
emergent curriculum   59-60
emotional intelligence   vi, 22, 44, 50-52, 58, 64-65, 138,
Emotional Quotient (EQ)   49
emotions   5, 6, 8, 20, 38, 41, 44, 45, 62, 63, 65, 81, 82, 93, 155,
Enlightenment, The   212
ethical choice(s)   32-33
evolutionary activism   71, 73
Extinction Rebellion   3, 9,
Facebook   3, 5, 110
Farnham, John   118
Finland, education system   59-60
First Nations, cultural traditions   37, 41
Flory, Vicki   64
flow-states   60-61, 138, 139
Fox, Josh   7
Fridays for Future   9
Ghandi, Mahatma   90
global transition   vi, 104,
global warming   6, 72
Google   110, 135, 160
GPS (global positioning system)   145
Happiness Professor   159
HeartMath Institute   79, 81
Hero's Journey, The   171
Higgins, Polly   viii
Holmes, Sharyn   viii
homework   40, 58, 137
ideator   142
Indigenous traditions   73, 94, 95, 101, 113
Instagram   110

Intergovernmental Panel on Climate Change   6
International Democratic Education Conference   59
intuition   70, 77-78, 80, 84, 86
intuitive intelligence   77-78, 80-86
King, Dr Martin Luther   89
Kulin nation   120
lightworkers   93
Macy, Joanne   vii
Melbourne Cricket Ground   38
menarche (rite of passage)   170
mental health, consequences   14, 48, 58, 63, 77, 159
microaggressions   97, 102
mindfulness   vi, 173,
Monbiot, George   viii, 37
multiculturalism   104, 106
Muslim, refugee   119
NAPLAN (National Assessment Program — Literacy and Numeracy)   140
Nazism   54
neoliberalism   54
neurodiversity   77
Nobel Prize   54
nutrition, quality   33
Obama, President Barak   123
Oprah, Winfrey   123
Our Children's Trust   21
parenting plans, development of   164-165, 174
Peck, M Scott   160, 171
people of colour, marginalisation of   94-98
positive change   vi, vii, 22, 31, 46, 85, 103, 104, 112, 155
Posselt, Steve   2

PTSD (Post-Traumatic stress Disorder) 14, 52, 63
pregnancy 69-71, 76-77
Project Oxygen 145
Puffing Billy 54
refugeeism vii, 135
refugees vii, 119, 140, 141,
resilience 34, 44, 49, 50-64, 94, 113, 134, 138, 159, 161, 164, 165, 172,
rites of passage 163, 170-174
rituals, development of 30, 37, 38, 44, 91, 164-166
RSPCA (Royal Society for the Prevention of Cruelty to Animals) 168
Saad, Layla viii
School Strikes for Climate 4, 15,
schoolies week 164
self-healing 91
social engagement 22
Southern Christian Leadership Conference 89
Spiritual Activism 85-86
Stalinism 54
standardised testing 145
STEM (science, technology, engineering, and maths) 45, 136, 140
TEDx talk 104
Third Culture Kids 104
Thunberg, Greta 3, 85, 150
Tomashauser, Regina 7
trampolines, risk 161-162
transport, convenience of 32-33
Trump, President Donald 124
trust 51, 68, 70-73, 83-86
Twitter 3, 5, 110
United Nations General Assembly 18
white saviour complex 99
white supremacy 93, 99, 100, 108
whitesplaining 96
wildlife extinction 31
World Economic Forum 13
World Heath Organization 50
Yousafzai, Malala 150
Zero Hour 3

This book has been produced on the stolen land of the Kulin Nation – Indigenous sovereignty has never been ceded. Radiate acknowledges the traditional custodians of the land, sea and waters where we live, work, and raise our families. We pay our respects to Elders past, present and emerging, who remain strong in their enduring connection to land and culture. We recognise the intrinsic link between colonisation and the problematic present and future upon which this book is based.

www.radiatepublishing.com

@radiatepublishing

@radiate.publishing

@radiatepublish1

www.ingramcontent.com/pod-product-compliance
Lightning Source LLC
Chambersburg PA
CBHW051945290426
44110CB00015B/2123